the BEEF CLUB

A BOOK FOR MEAT LOVERS

Creators of The Beef Club: Pierre-Charles Cros, Romée de Goriainoff and Olivier Bon,
Jean Moueix and Nicolas Chevalier. Special thanks to Keda Black
Photographs by Marie-Pierre Morel

the BEEF CLUB

hardie grant books
MELBOURNE · LONDON

FOREWORD

The French may be great carnivores – it's normal for us to eat meat every day – but quantity seems to have taken precedence over quality. Intensive rearing, the complexity of the meat industry, and butchery practices that perhaps are not as good as they used to be, seem to have sounded the death knell for the true taste of beef.

It is to this true taste that we have dedicated The Beef Club, in the fashion of American-style restaurants and in the tradition of the 'Beefsteak Clubs' that emerged in London at the beginning of the 18th century. At the most famous of them, 'The Sublime Society of Beef Steaks', its members (artists, aristocrats, politicians, military men and even royalty) gathered every Saturday afternoon and were regaled with vast quantities of beef. In a very 'down-to-earth' spirit, the meat was washed down only with strong drinks such as porter or punch (the ancestor of the modern cocktail): French-style fine wines were considered an affectation of a clique of aristocrats who were more concerned with the arts and foreign food than the produce of their native soil.

In Paris, we know that there's nothing prententious in the way French wine complements the flavour of a fine meat, and we have of course an excellent wine list at The Beef Club. But we decided to also keep alive the tradition of offering a selection of cocktails, which we serve in the Ballroom (the restaurant's bar in the basement), in spirit of the English establishments that inspired it. And even if the ambience is a little more elegant and less masculine than that of the early English beefsteak clubs or American steakhouses, we have set out to make The Beef Club a friendly place serving delicious food. On the menu are generous dishes for sharing, in a true coming together of French and British traditions.

Everything is centred on meat at its very best: from animals reared and slaughtered with thought; the meat cut and matured by experienced butchers, and then cooked with great skill. Each of these stages is carried out with the expertise that lies at the heart of our restaurant's success. We hope this book will reflect this, and that it will encourage you to choose and eat – less frequently if necessary – better meat.

the BENCH
CLUB

CONTENTS

EXPERTISE

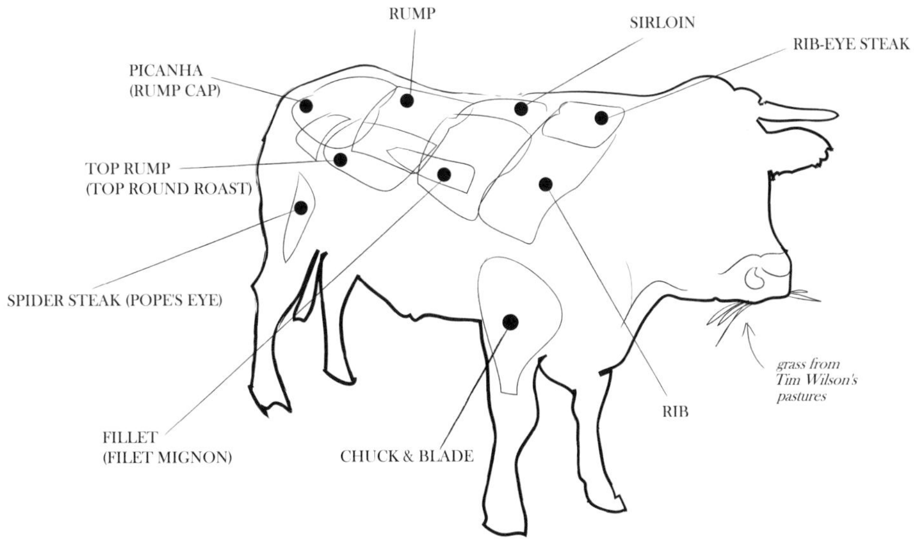
RUMP
SIRLOIN
RIB-EYE STEAK
PICANHA
(RUMP CAP)
TOP RUMP
(TOP ROUND ROAST)
SPIDER STEAK (POPE'S EYE)
FILLET
(FILET MIGNON)
CHUCK & BLADE
RIB
grass from
Tim Wilson's
pastures

FARMED
in the heart of
NORTH YORKSHIRE

OUR MEAT AT THE BEEF CLUB COMES DIRECTLY FROM YORKSHIRE, FROM THE GINGER PIG FARM WHERE TIM WILSON REARS HIS COWS.

A global approach

When we were developing our 'steak house' project, we soon ran into a problem. Very few French cattle breeders produce meat that is high in quality, suitable for grilling and, above all, available constantly in sufficient quantity. On a trip to England we met Tim Wilson, one of the world's most renowned cattle farmers.

Ginger Pig

The name of his farm comes from a rare breed of pig kept by very few farmers. A great enthusiast for British native breeds, Tim wasn't content with merely raising animals. He has revolutionised farming methods, brought back old and cross-breeds, and established his own chain of butcher's shops in London where his meat is sold. The Ginger Pig farm has around 5,000 animals (cattle, pigs and sheep) of various breeds dating from the 19th century, which are smaller, more active and better suited to cooking on the grill. Some say that his farming is closer to an art than it is to agriculture...

The green meadows of North Yorkshire

As both farmer and butcher, Tim has his eye on the entire supply chain. His farming is designed to obtain the best possible meat while treating the animals with respect. His farm is in Yorkshire, among the grassy meadows of northern England; located away from roads and towns, it is protected from all kinds of pollution. His animals live outdoors, in wide open spaces where they feed on rich grass and some grains: 100 per cent natural food, with no antibiotics. Tim oversees his animals throughout their life, ensuring minimum stress at slaughter time. His approach is to cut out the middleman between farm and plate; at The Beef Club, we receive a delivery once a week, directly from his farm. We know what we're putting on our plate.

CATTLE *from Yorkshire* TO THE BEEF CLUB

ON HIS GINGER PIG FARM, TIM WILSON RAISES HIS CATTLE WITH PASSION. WE TRUST HIS KNOW-HOW AND EXPERTISE TO GUARANTEE LOVERS OF GOOD MEAT THE VERY FINEST QUALITY.

The breeds

Tim rears four main breeds of cow. He believes that each breed is suited to a particular region and type of land and he selects them on this basis. But he also told us that when he began farming, he chose Longhorn cattle for their beauty, and admits that he likes to have beautiful animals in his meadows! His other breeds are Shorthorns, Herefords and Galloways. Breeding his cattle and rearing the calves – they are kept with their mothers for at least ten months, then slowly allowed to reach maturity – requires a great deal of knowledge, skill and hard work.

None of his animals are slaughtered before the age of 18 months (and often not before 24 months), an eternity (and a rarity) in the current farming world. In his view, this is the time needed to allow the animals to reach maturity and to develop that essential layer of fat that gives the meat its exceptional flavour, which differs according to the breed.

Good meat

After speaking with Tim, we learned that good meat comes first and foremost from good farming. We should always find out about the meat we eat: what breed the animal is, what it has been fed, how long has it been given to mature before slaughter and how long it has been aged.

These are the questions that we should ask when buying meat, and which for us always call for the same answers: a traditional breed suited to the region where it lives, which has been grass-fed and allowed to mature until 30 months old, and hung for at least 28 days. This is the type of meat that we bring to The Beef Club, direct from Yorkshire.

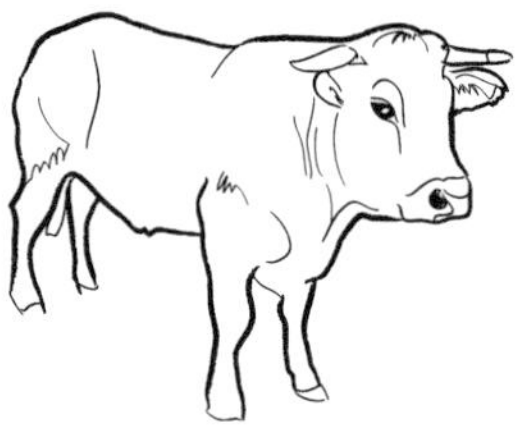

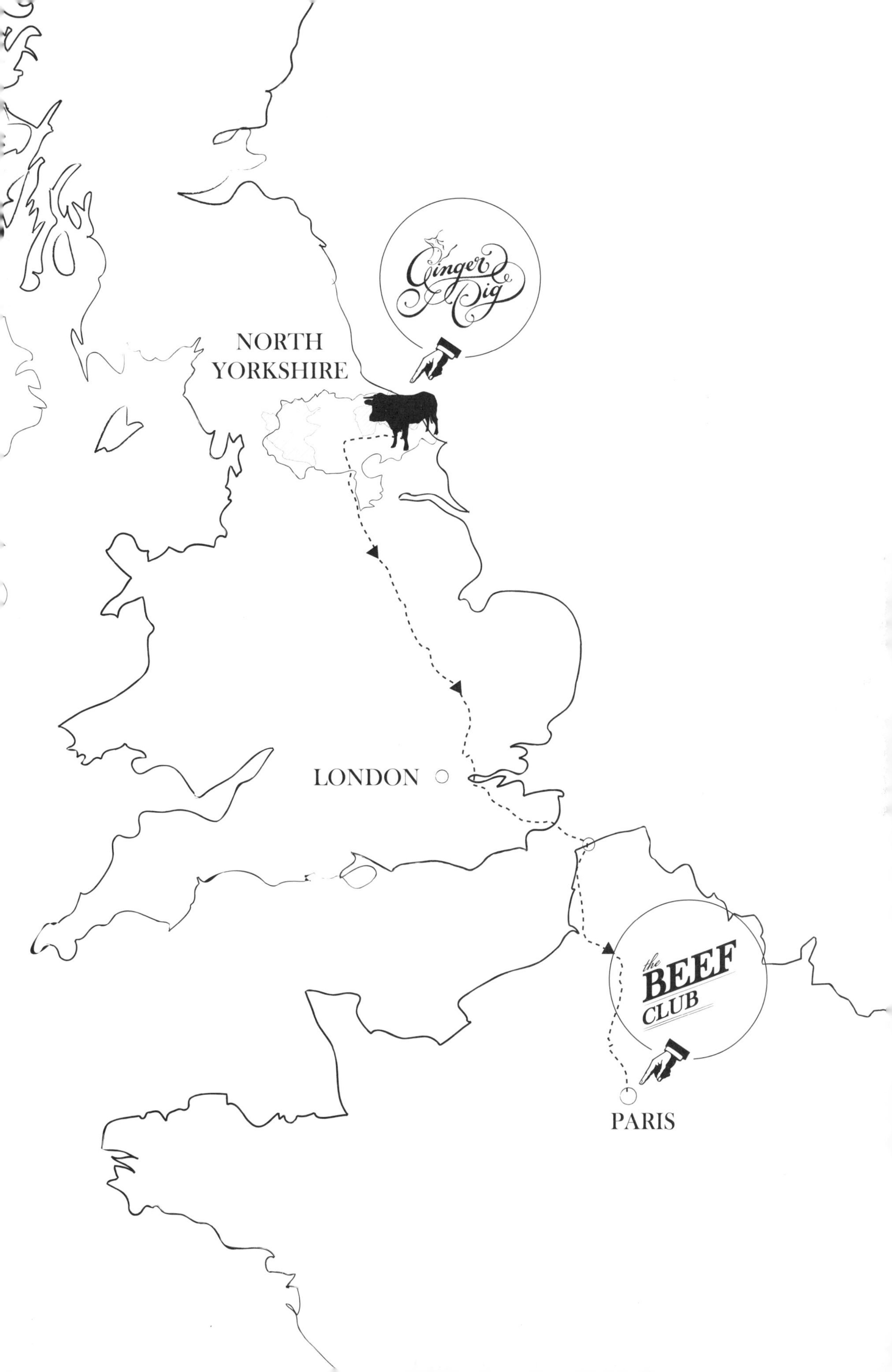
Ginger Pig
NORTH YORKSHIRE
LONDON
the BEEF CLUB
PARIS

YORKSHIRE

Cow Country

THE BEEF CLUB
The Cold Room

EXPERTISE

BUTCHERY
AND AGEING
of the Meat

WE MATURE OUR BEEF FOR AT LEAST TWENTY DAYS IN ORDER TO GIVE IT THE BEST FLAVOUR. AFTER SLAUGHTER, THE MEAT IS HUNG IN A COLD ROOM WHERE THE TEMPERATURE IS MAINTAINED AT BETWEEN 0–2°C (32–36°F); THE HANGING PERIOD DEPENDS ON THE BREED, CUT AND HOW WE INTEND TO COOK THE BEEF.

At The Beef Club

It is normal for a traditional butcher to allow the meat to rest for at least a few days after slaughter. At The Beef Club we have chosen to hang the meat ourselves.

From the farm to our cold room

Our meat comes directly from The Ginger Pig farm. Tim, who is a butcher as well as a farmer, slaughters and stores the beef in a cold room in order to start the dry ageing process, which we continue after it has been delivered to us. Tim knows that our needs change depending on how busy we are and always keeps a 'buffer' stock for when our demand increases. Our meat is usually delivered to us by Tim himself, but if not he sends a member of his team. When Tim comes to Paris he often brings us other English artisanal products such as cheeses and takes home French produce, which he sells in his Ginger Pig shops. While he's here he also casts an expert eye over our beef during the dry ageing process.

Cutting

Once or twice a week a butcher will come to prepare the different cuts of meat – ribs, rib-eye and rump steaks, etc. – for us from our matured beef. This is a big job and takes several hours. Here at The Beef Club we grill our meat and the most suitable cuts for this are taken from the hind end of the animal where the muscles have worked moderately during the animal's life. In contrast, the fore-end is very muscular and the cuts taken from here are more suitable for long, slow cooking. The cuts from the middle of the beef are the most tender as the muscles here have done very little work, so the meat can be cooked quickly and kept very rare.

Dry-ageing at the restaurant

The meat is kept at a constant temperature in a protected environment – our purpose-built cold room. During the maturing process the moisture evaporates from the beef and it develops an outer crust, which helps to tenderise and concentrate the flavour of the meat. Once the beef has been aged for the required amount of time, the butcher meticulously trims away the crust, resulting in a reduction of around 30 per cent of the weight.

And at home?

Dry ageing meat is a craft and should only be done by experienced professionals and not at home. Although cooking destroys most bacteria, if the meat isn't carefully monitored it can still present risks. Dividing the meat into the various different cuts also requires great skill. So, to enjoy well-aged beef buy it from a butcher who matures his meat for at least 28 days or eat at a restaurant that serves it. Thanks to our close ties with Tim and the butchers we use, and our careful dry ageing process, we serve choice cuts that have been aged for four to six weeks. For some customers we even extend the maturing period to 90 days. All this is what gives our beef an incomparable flavour.

DRY AGEING

AFTER AGEING *the meat*

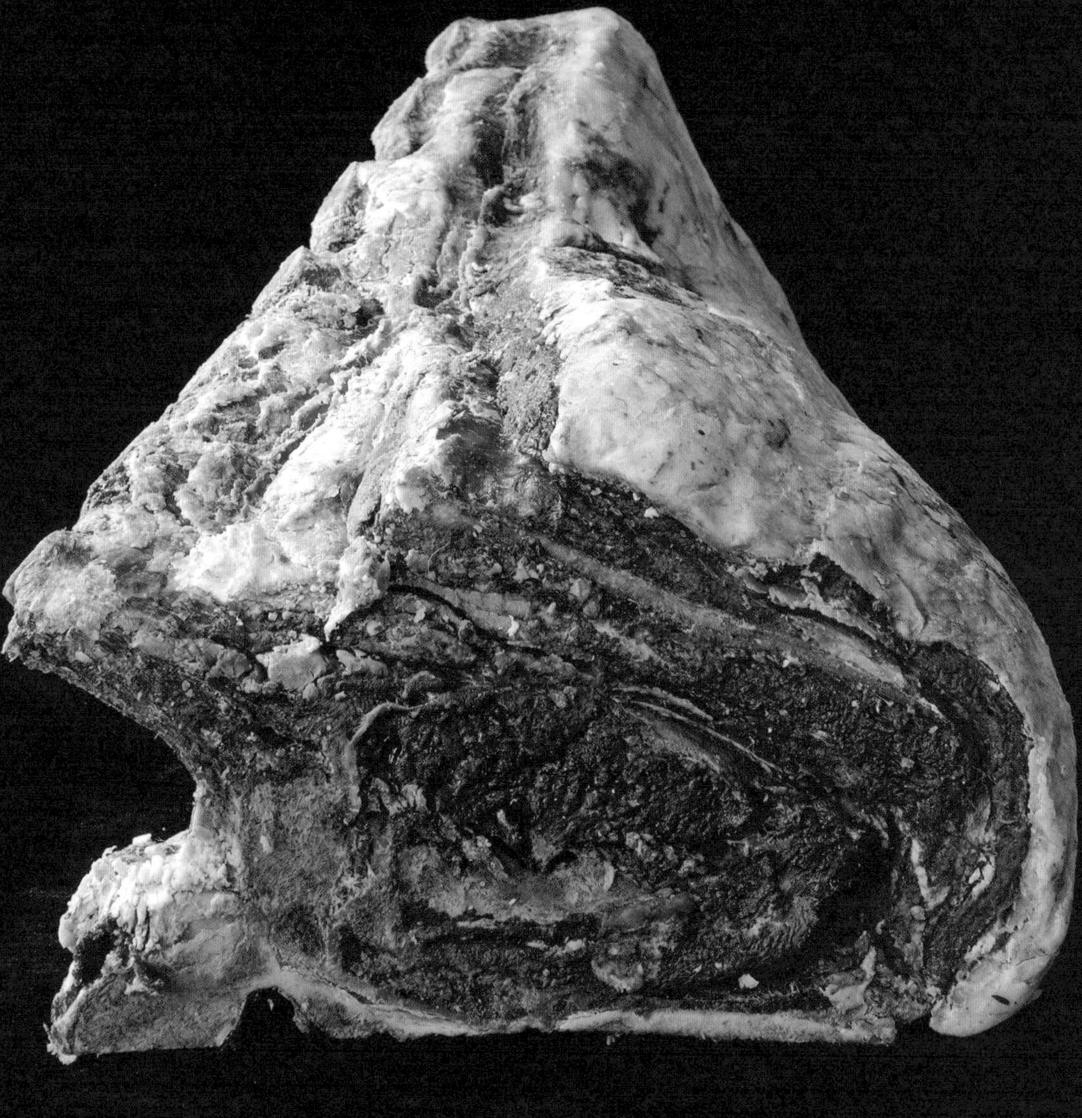

READY TO COOK

AFTER THE BUTCHER'S *work*

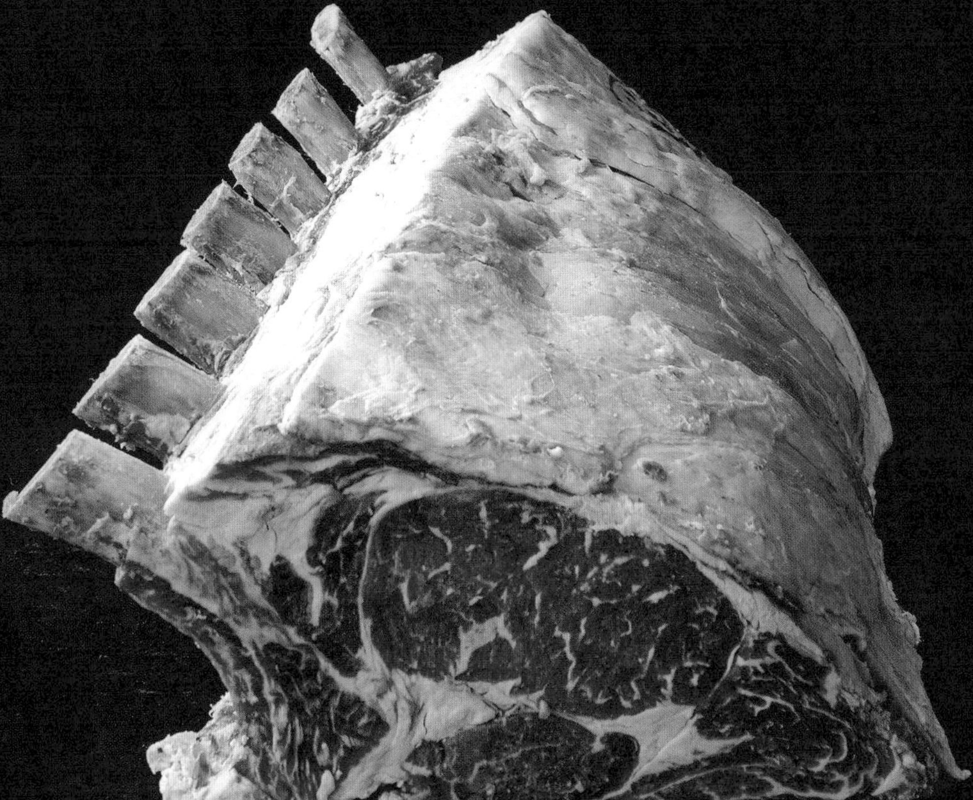

COOKING
THE BEEF

AFTER AGEING AND CUTTING, COOKING IS THE KEY STAGE IN PREPARING MEAT. AT THE BEEF CLUB WE USE A WOOD OVEN, WHICH ALLOWS US TO ACHIEVE VERY HIGH COOKING TEMPERATURES, FOR PERFECTLY SEARED MEAT.

So who is Josper?

Our trademark is cooking over charcoal. We use a Josper oven, which is a Spanish brand that is an oven and barbecue grill combined. It doesn't run on electricity but is instead fired entirely by charcoal. We cook the meat over the hot coals once the flames have died down. There is an adjustable vent system that allows air inside and circulates the smoke, giving us greater control over the temperature, with highs of up to 400°C (750°F). This is ideal for searing and caramelizing the meat on the outside, while keeping it very rare inside. You can cook everything on it, including vegetables, fish and shellfish. This traditional cooking method, using modern equipment, gives our food a truly unique flavour while retaining its natural qualities.

At home

With domestic equipment, whether cooking in the oven or on the barbecue, just as much care must be taken in a professional kitchen.

Cooking according to cut

At the restaurant, we cook our beef on the barbecue. You should do the same at home whenever possible, otherwise it is best to use a cast iron griddle pan or frying pan on the stove top, or cook it in the oven. It is important to adapt how you cook the meat according to the cut you are using, ensuring it is 'nourished' either by its own fat or by adding fat or liquid to ensure it doesn't dry out. The natural flavour of the beef should be respected, but can be subtly enhanced or even spiced up with herbs, spices and condiments. Your butcher will be able to advise you on what is the best age and cut of meat to get for how you intend to cook it.

There is no such thing as the perfect cut of meat: the most tender will be the least tasty and the tastier ones will have a firmer bite. It is also a matter of personal preference. There are meats for the trendy, for the snob, for the wise, for cowboys… It's up to you to try them and find your own favourite cuts of beef. The cuts shown on the next pages are mainly intended for short, rapid cooking, and are at their best served rare…

Core temperatures of the meat:

Temperature for very rare meat: 50°C (120°F).

Temperature for rare meat: 55°C (130°F).

Temperature for medium meat: 60°C (140°F).

Temperature for well-done meat: 70–75°C (160–170°F).

COOKING
ACCORDING TO THE CUT

RIB OF BEEF

As its name suggests, the rib comes from the fore-end of the animal. It is a cut that is suitable for roasting as it contains a layer of fat to 'nourish' it well during cooking. This fat and the fact that it is cooked on the bone give it a lot of flavour… Of course, the rib is also perfect for the barbecue. Try it with a Pumpkin Boulangère (page 166).

The cut
The rib of beef is towards the back of the fore-end of the animal, between the neck and the sirloin.

The butcher's choice
A well-marbled rib. 1 kg (2 lb 3 oz) serves 2 people.

The Beef Club's advice
The rib should be tender, juicy and fatty, with a more powerful flavour close to the bone. It is the cut that offers the broadest flavour palette. Take care to take the rib out of the fridge 1 hour before cooking so as not to shock the meat.

RIB-EYE STEAK

This is not really from in between the ribs, yet is the same cut as the rib, but deboned. So it has the same kind of properties: fairly tender (as it comes from muscles that work only moderately in the lifetime of the animal) and fairly marbled (although this depends on the farming practices). On the other hand, the absence of bone changes how you cook it, which makes it more an individual than a group cut (although again this depends on the animal and on the butcher). Serve with a nice marrowbone stock, mmmm!

The cut
Rib-eye is also from the fore part of the animal's back, but without the bones.

The butcher's choice
A nicely marbled rib-eye, thick and squat so it can be cooked beautifully. Use 250–300 g (9–10½ oz) per rib-eye 2–3 cm (¾–1¼ in) thick.

The Beef Club's advice
Don't hesitate to choose a fatty piece, the fat will feed moisture to the meat while it cooks.

SIRLOIN

Another lean cut, nice and tender, with tight fibres, the texture of which must be respected by quick cooking. Serve with a strongly flavoured accompaniment such as Black Turnips or radicchio (pages 172 and 174).

The cut
The sirloin is between the ribs and the rump. It is one of the superior cuts.

The butcher's choice
A juicy, tender sirloin, slightly marbled with fat. 250–350 g (9–12 oz) per sirloin 2–2.5 cm (¾–1 in) thick.

The Beef Club's advice
Remove the gristle but leave the covering of fat.

FILLET

This cut is highly prized because it comes from a muscle that works little and therefore produces a very tender meat. Because it is not fatty it has the reputation of being a lady's steak. It is delicious rare, served with a tasty sauce such as stilton (page 58).

The cut
The fillet comes from the back of the animal, level with the lumbar vertebrae.

The butcher's choice
A cut that has little fat and delicate fibres, elegant with a sweet flavour. Use 180–220 g (6–8 oz) per fillet.

The Beef Club's advice
Mature the fillet in order to give it a stronger flavour. Ask your butcher to do this for you.

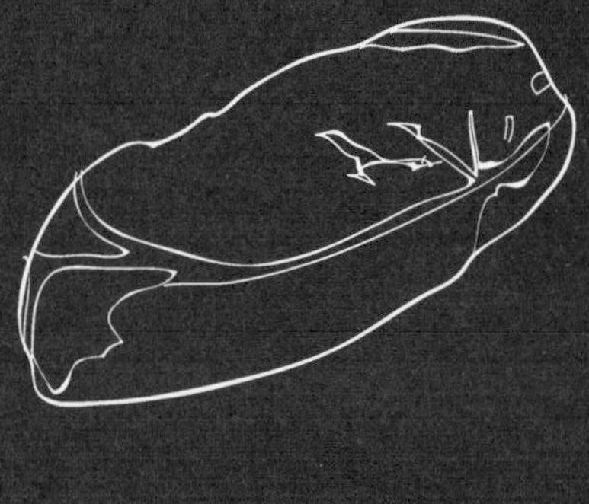

RUMP

The steak for the real steak lover: full of flavour with a nice firm bite. It is taken from the rump of the animal. It must be aged well. It is best fairly thick (5 cm/2 in), cooked relatively quickly on a very powerful heat source and cut into fine strips.

The cut
From the rear of the animal, between the sirloin and the rump, it carries little fat and has long fibres.

The butcher's choice
A nice thick rump steak is a very juicy cut with a powerful flavour. Use 180–220 g (6–8 oz) per rump steak 3–4 cm (1¼–1¾ in) thick.

The Beef Club's advice
Retain the covering of fat.

TOP RUMP

Yet another of this group of really tasty steaks, this is a very tender cut, low in fat. It is firmer in the mouth than a fillet steak but also has more flavour! Serve with a Béarnaise Sauce and Potato Wedges (pages 56 and 140), of course.

The cut
It is close to the rump, separated by gristle.

The butcher's choice
A lean cut. Use 180–220 g (6–8 oz) per medallion 3–4 cm (1¼–1¾ in) thick.

The Beef Club's advice
Cut into thick medallions.

PICANHA/RUMP-CAP

Picanha, more commonly known as the rump cap, is a Brazilian or Argentinian cut. Taken from the upper base of the tail, it is a tender and marbled cut, which is best suited for cooking on a barbecue as it brings out the flavours of the meat. It is also used in steak tartare.

The cut
Taken from the top of the rump with its layer of fat left on and is cut against the grain of the fibre.

The butcher's choice
A picanha with a high muscle/fat ratio cut from a well-aged animal. Use 220–300 g (8–10½ oz) per picanha.

The Beef Club's advice
A cut for real meat lovers!

ROYAL

This is the king, and yet it is not very well known! Indeed the name relates mainly to a very little-known cut applied to precious, tasty areas of the rump. A royal cut needs royal cooking. This rare cut needs a cook as skilful as the butcher who trims it. It deserves a fine accompaniment such as well buttered spinach as it is rather lean.

The cut
It comes from the area between the sirloin and the rump. It's a thick slice of sirloin that has had its covering of fat completely removed along with any gristle.

The butcher's choice
A nicely marbled royal, tender and flavoursome. Use 600–800 g (1 lb 5 oz–1 lb 12 oz), then cut into 200–400 g (7–14 oz) pieces.

The Beef Club's advice
It must be watched closely, as it's a cut that requires special attention during cooking.

SPIDER STEAK/POPE'S EYE

A popular cut in France, this is our name for a 300-400 g (10½–14 oz) cut with a web of marbled fat. Not particularly attractive to look at but delicious, they remind us of what French butchers call '*araignée*' (one piece of the animal's groin, formed from one main piece and eight long spider like pieces – hence the name). Tender and tasty, these cuts are grilled rare and eaten with a sauce and a garnish that is not too elaborate.

The cut
Langue de chat, which is in the rump – a small very juicy muscle with a firm texture.
The 'tail' of the fillet, which is the pointed end of the tenderloin.
The side strap or chain of the tenderloin or fillet – this is a fibrous muscle on the fillet.

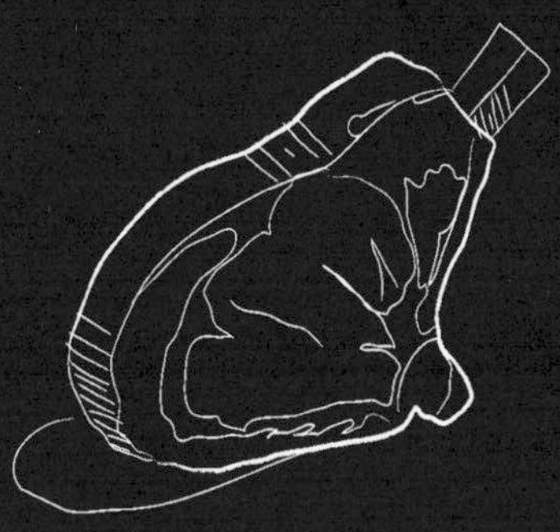

BLEU
A POINT

BIEN CUIT
A POINT
SAIGNANT

BARBECUE

RIB
of Beef

Cooking times vary according to preference

SERVES 2

INGREDIENTS

1 rib of beef weighing 1 kg (2 lb 3 oz)
100 ml (3½ fl oz) olive oil
sea salt and freshly ground black pepper
60 g (2 oz) fresh butter (if using)

COOKING TIME

5 minutes each side
for very rare to rare

10 minutes each side
for medium

15–20 minutes each side
for well done

ON THE BARBECUE OVER HOT COALS

Before cooking, cover the rib with olive oil and season with salt and pepper.

Adjust the cooking time according to how you like your meat done.

IN A FRYING OR SAUTÉ PAN

Season the rib with salt and pepper. Brown on both sides in olive oil over a high heat.

Add the butter and lower the heat.

Baste with the butter throughout cooking. Take care not to let the butter burn; it should stay pale in colour and nice and foamy.

AFTER COOKING

Let the rib rest for at least 15 minutes. This resting time allows the flesh to relax and the juices to be reabsorbed into the meat.

TIP

For perfectly seasoned meat, massage the rib with salt before cooking to help it penetrate.

RIB-EYE STEAK

Cooking times vary according to preference

SERVES 1

INGREDIENTS

1 rib-eye steak weighing 300 g (10½ oz)
50 ml (2 fl oz) olive oil
sea salt and freshly ground black pepper
40 g (1½ oz) fresh butter (if using)

COOKING TIME

1–2 minutes each side for very rare to rare

2–3 minutes each side for medium

5 minutes each side for well done

ON THE BARBECUE OVER HOT COALS

Before cooking, cover the rib-eye with olive oil, and season with salt and pepper.

Adjust the cooking time according to how you like your meat done.

IN A FRYING OR SAUTÉ PAN

Season the rib-eye with salt and pepper. Brown on both sides in olive oil over a high heat.

Add the butter and lower the heat.

Baste with the butter throughout cooking. Take care not to let the butter burn; it should stay pale in colour and nice and foamy.

SIRLOIN

Cooking times vary according to preference

SERVES 1

INGREDIENTS

1 sirloin steak weighing 300 g (10½ oz)
50 ml (2 fl oz) olive oil
sea salt and freshly ground black pepper
40 g (1½ oz) fresh butter (if using)

COOKING TIME

1–2 minutes each side
for very rare to rare

2–3 minutes each side
for medium

5 minutes each side
for well done

ON THE BARBECUE OVER HOT COAL

Oil the sirloin with olive oil before cooking, season with salt and pepper. Score the fat to enable the heat to penetrate and prevent the meat from curling up.

Adjust the cooking time for the type of grill required.

IN A FRYING OR SAUTÉ PAN

Season the sirloin with salt and pepper. Brown on both sides in olive oil over a high heat. Lightly score the fat to prevent the meat from curling up.

Add the butter and lower the heat.

Baste with the butter throughout cooking. Take care not to let the butter burn; it should stay pale in colour and nice and foamy.

FILLET
Steak

Cooking times vary according to preference

SERVES 1

INGREDIENTS

1 fillet steak weighing 200 g (7 oz)
50 ml (2 fl oz) olive oil
sea salt and freshly ground
black pepper
40 g (1½ oz) fresh butter (if using)

COOKING TIME

3 minutes each side
for very rare to rare

5 minutes each side
for medium

6 minutes each side
for well done

ON THE BARBECUE OVER HOT COALS

Cover the fillet steak with olive oil before cooking so that it doesn't dry out. Season with salt and pepper.

Adjust the cooking time according to how you like your meat done.

IN A FRYING OR SAUTÉ PAN

Season the fillet steak with salt and pepper. Brown on both sides in olive oil over a high heat.

Add the butter and lower the heat.

Baste with the butter throughout cooking. Take care not to let the butter burn; it should stay pale in colour and nice and foamy.

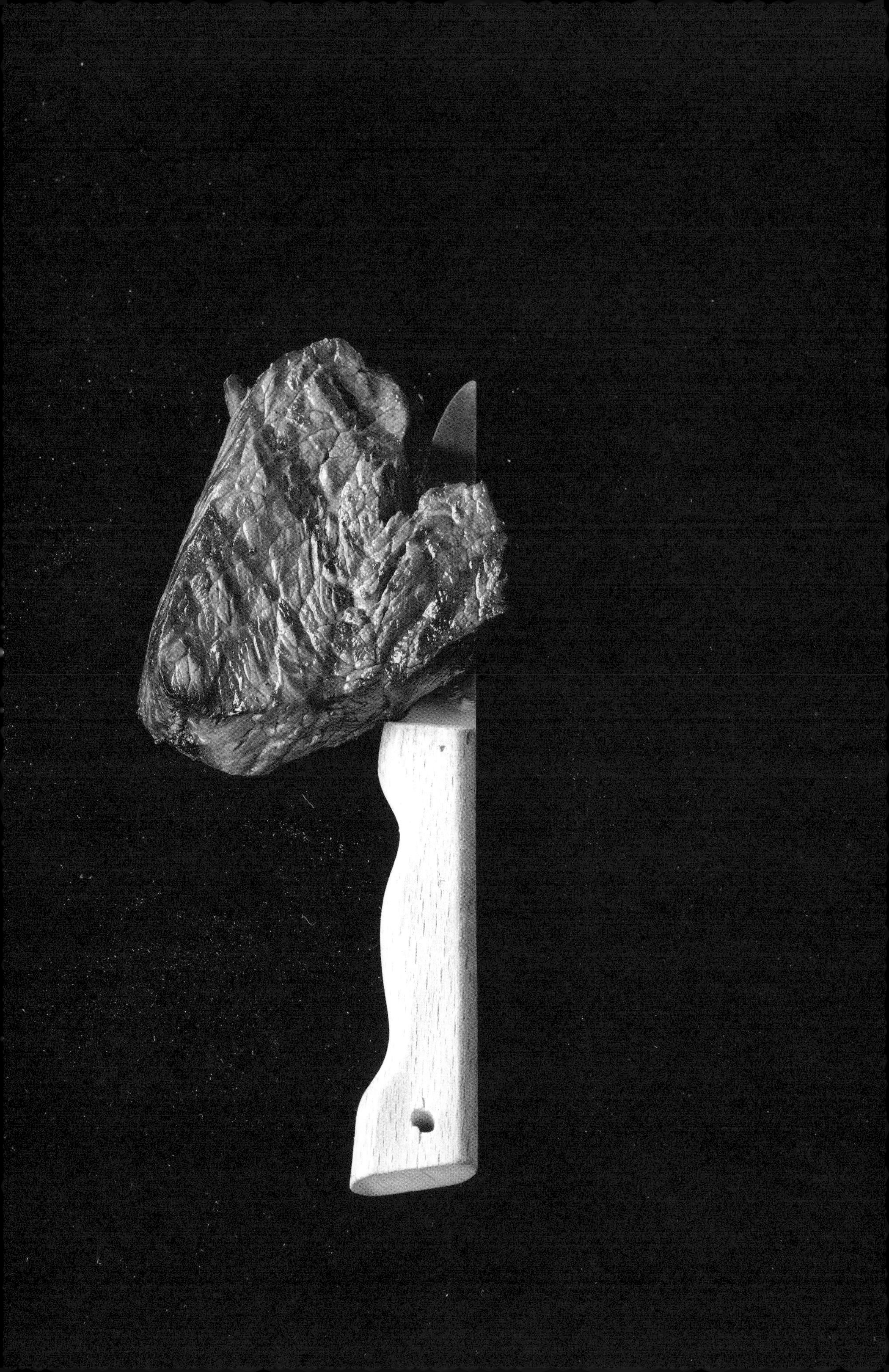

RUMP
Steak

Cooking times vary according to preference

SERVES 1

INGREDIENTS

1 rump steak weighing 200 g (7 oz)
50 ml (2 fl oz) olive oil
sea salt and freshly ground black pepper
40 g (1½ oz) fresh butter (if using)

COOKING TIME

2 minutes each side
for very rare to rare

4 minutes each side
for medium,

4 minutes each side
for well done (halve the steak lengthwise then cook)

also delicious raw as steak tartare

ON THE BARBECUE OVER HOT COALS

Cover the rump steak with olive oil before cooking. Season with salt and pepper.

Adjust the cooking time according to how you like your meat done.

IN A FRYING PAN OR SAUTÉ PAN

Season the rump steak with salt and pepper. Brown on both sides in olive oil over a high heat.

Add the butter and lower the heat.

Baste with the butter throughout cooking. Take care not to let the butter burn; it should stay pale in colour and nice and foamy.

11

FILLET
OF
RUMP STEAK

Cooking times vary according to preference

SERVES 1

INGREDIENTS

1 fillet of rump steak weighing 200 g (7 oz)
50 ml (2 fl oz) olive oil
sea salt and freshly ground black pepper
40 g (1½ oz) fresh butter (if using)

COOKING TIME

2 minutes each side
for very rare to rare

4 minutes each side
for medium

4 minutes each side
for well done (halve the medallion lengthwise then cook)

ON THE BARBECUE OVER HOT COALS

Cover the fillet of rump steak with olive oil. Season with salt and pepper. Adjust the cooking time according to how you like your meat done.

IN A FRYING OR SAUTÉ PAN

Season the fillet of rump steak with salt and pepper. Brown on both sides in olive oil over a high heat.

Add the butter and lower the heat.

The meat should be cooked gently to prevent it drying out.

Baste with the butter throughout cooking. Take care not to let the butter burn; it should stay pale in colour and nice and foamy.

PICANHA (RUMP CAP)

Cooking times vary according to preference

SERVES 1

INGREDIENTS

1 picanha weighing 250 g (9 oz)
50 ml (2 fl oz) olive oil
sea salt and freshly ground black pepper
40 g (1½ oz) fresh butter (if using)

COOKING TIME

2 minutes each side
for very rare to rare

3 minutes each side,
then rest for 5 minutes
for medium

delicious raw as tartare – not recommended for eating well done

ON THE BARBECUE OVER HOT COALS

Cover the picanha with olive oil. Season with salt and pepper.

Adjust the cooking time according to how you like your meat done.

IN A FRYING OR SAUTÉ PAN

Season the picanha with salt and pepper. Brown on both sides in olive oil over a high heat.

Add the butter and lower the heat. Baste with the butter throughout cooking. Take care not to let the butter burn.

ROYAL

Cooking times vary according to preferences

SERVES 1

INGREDIENTS

1 royal weighing 250 g (9 oz)
50 ml (2 fl oz) olive oil
sea salt and freshly ground black pepper
40 g (1½ oz) fresh butter (if using)

COOKING TIME

1–2 minutes each side for very rare to rare

2–3 minutes each side for medium

5 minutes each side for well done

ON THE BARBECUE OVER HOT COALS

Cover the royal with olive oil. Season with salt and pepper.

Adjust the cooking time according to how you like your meat done. Keep a close eye on the meat while cooking because as the cut is irregular, heat can penetrate very quickly.

IN A FRYING OR SAUTÉ PAN

Season the royal with salt and pepper. Brown on both sides in olive oil over a high heat.

Add the butter and lower the heat.

Baste with the butter throughout cooking. Keep a close eye the meat while cooking because as the cut is irregular, heat can penetrate very quickly.

SPIDER (POPE'S EYE) *Steak*

Cooking times vary according to preference

THE SIZE OF CUT IS VARIABLE

INGREDIENTS

langue de chat or
tail of the fillet or
side strap or chain of the fillet

These cuts are not particularly attractive to look at, and you won't find them on your butcher's counter (butchers prefer to keep them for use in other recipes). They are, however, delicious. Don't hesitate to ask for them, it's the only way you will get them. The size of these cuts varies from one animal to another, which makes it difficult to state a cooking time. However, we recommend you cook them rare to medium-rare to fully appreciate their flavours.

BÉARNAISE
Sauce

Preparation 20 minutes / Cooking 15 minutes

SERVES 4–6

INGREDIENTS

2 shallots
1½ bunches of tarragon
1 teaspoon crushed peppercorns
(not ground too fine)
100 ml (3½ fl oz) spirit vinegar
100 ml (3½ fl oz) white wine
250 g (9 oz) unsalted butter
4 egg yolks
2 tablespoons cold water
1 bunch of chives

Peel and finely slice the shallots and chop 1 bunch of tarragon. Mix both together with the crushed peppercorns in a saucepan.

Add the vinegar and wine, bring to a simmer and reduce down to 3–4 tablespoons of liquid.

Strain and set aside (discard the shallots, pepper and tarragon).

Melt the butter over a low heat in a small saucepan. Remove from the heat and skim off the white foam from the surface with a spoon. Gently pour the butter into a bowl, leaving behind the solids deposited on the bottom of the saucepan. It doesn't matter if a little of this goes in the butter.

Put the egg yolks into a heatproof bowl and place on top of a saucepan of boiling water without letting the bowl touch the water.

Whisk in the wine and vinegar reduction, along with the water, then whisk in the clarified butter. Chop and add the rest of the tarragon and the chives.

Keep the sauce warm over the water until you are ready to serve, whisk again before serving.

NOTE

Butter is clarified to remove the milk solids and water, leaving only the butterfat; as a result the butter can be heated to a higher temperature without burning, or used in an emulsion.

TIP

If the egg yolks curdle and the sauce separates, sit the bowl in a container of cold water, add a spoonful of hot water and whisk vigorously.

STILTON
Sauce

Preparation 5 minutes / Cooking 10 minutes

SERVES 4–6

INGREDIENTS

250 g (9 oz) full-fat single (half-and-half) cream
250 g (9 oz) thick (heavy) cream
200 g (7 oz) Stilton (or other blue cheese)
freshly ground pepper
¼ bunch of chives

Mix the 2 creams together in a saucepan, place over a gentle heat, stir and allow to reduce slowly by half until you have a thick smooth consistency. Crumble in the Stilton and stir until it melts. Season with black pepper.

Before serving, sprinkle with chopped chives. The sauce is best served immediately, but can be kept in the fridge and reheated gently before serving.

CHIMICHURRI

Sauce

Preparation 20 minutes

SERVES 4–6

INGREDIENTS

- 1 bunch of coriander (cilantro)
- 1 bunch of parsley
- 100 ml (3½ fl oz) olive oil
- 100 ml (3½ fl oz) grapeseed oil
- 2 large ripe tomatoes
- 1 red onion
- 1 small chilli pepper
- 2 garlic cloves
- 1 teaspoon dried oregano
- ½ teaspoon ground cumin
- 1 teaspoon paprika
- 1 teaspoon salt
- juice of ½ a lemon
- 4 tablespoons chardonnay vinegar (or other white wine vinegar)
- 4 teaspoons sherry vinegar

Remove and discard the stalks from the coriander and parsley and finely chop the leaves. Pour the olive oil and grapeseed oil into a bowl and stir in the chopped fresh herbs.

Cut the tomatoes into approximately 2 mm (⅛ in) dice, peel and finely dice the onion and finely chop the chilli. Peel and finely grate the garlic. Mix the tomatoes, onion, chilli and garlic together in a bowl, then stir through the herby oil mixture. Add the oregano, cumin, paprika, salt, lemon juice, and chardonnay and sherry vinegars. Stir to combine

The sauce can be kept in the fridge for several hours, but should be taken out 30 minutes to an hour before serving (and preferably consumed the same day).

AÏOLI
Sauce

Preparation 10 minutes

SERVES 4–6

INGREDIENTS

2 egg yolks
1 teaspoon Dijon mustard
salt
200 ml (7 fl oz) sunflower oil
2 garlic cloves

Beat together the egg yolks, mustard and a pinch of salt in a bowl. Slowly pour the oil in, whisking vigorously. Continue by pouring in a thin trickle, without stopping whisking, to make the mayonnaise.

Purée the garlic and incorporate it into the mayonnaise.

Keep in the fridge and consume the same day.

If you like a touch of acidity, you can add a few drops of lemon juice at the beginning with the egg.

PEPPER
Sauce

Preparation 5 minutes (if the meat stock is already made) / Cooking 20 minutes

SERVES 6

INGREDIENTS

THE MEAT STOCK
1 kg (2 lb 3 oz)beef trimmings (ask your butcher for these)
1 kg (2 lb 3 oz) veal bones
1 tablespoon olive oil
1 carrot
2 onions
1 stick of celery
1 leek
2 tablespoons flour
1 teaspoon tomato purée (paste)
3 garlic cloves, peeled and chopped
2 bay leaves
1 sprig of thyme

THE PEPPER SAUCE
1 tablespoon olive oil
2 shallots
1 tablespoon crushed black pepper
1 tablespoon crushed Sarawak pepper (or failing that, ordinary black pepper)
1 tablespoon red Pondicherry pepper, or failing that, ordinary black pepper
50 ml (2 fl oz) cognac
2 tablespoons double (heavy) cream
salt

Make the meat stock according to the instructions on page 66.

Heat the oil in a frying pan and finely slice the shallots. Add them to the pan and sweat for 6–7 minutes over a medium heat until they are lightly browned. Add the 3 different types of pepper – or use 3 tablespoons of ordinary crushed black pepper if you can't find the Sarawak and Pondicherry peppercorns – and continue cooking for a further 1–2 minutes to roast them.

Pour in the cognac to deglaze the pan, scrape the bottom well and allow to boil and reduce right down.

Add 300 ml (10 fl oz) of meat stock, then add the cream. Reduce again at a gentle simmer until you have a nice creamy consistency. Season with a little salt.

BEEF MARROW STOCK *in red wine*

Preparation 3 days + 20 minutes / Cooking 4½ hours

SERVES 6

INGREDIENTS

BEEF STOCK
- 1 kg (2 lb 3 oz) beef trimmings (ask your butcher for these)
- 1 kg (2 lb 3 oz) veal bones
- 1 tablespoon olive oil
- 1 carrot
- 2 onions
- 1 stick of celery
- 1 leek
- 2 tablespoons flour
- 1 teaspoon tomato purée (paste)
- 3 garlic cloves, peeled and chopped
- 2 bay leaves
- 1 sprig of thyme

MARROW IN RED WINE SAUCE
- 2 large shallots
- 300 ml (10 fl oz) red wine (such as Côtes-du-Rhône or Languedoc)
- 30 g (1 oz) beef marrow
- 1 tablespoon olive oil
- 1 tablespoon red wine vinegar
- sea salt and freshly ground black pepper

Two days in advance, soak the marrow in cold water. Change the water each day. It should be clear at the end of the two days.

To make the stock, preheat the oven to 200°C. Put the beef trimmings and veal bones in an oven dish, sprinkle with olive oil and brown in the oven for 20–30 minutes.

In the meantime, wash, peel, and chop all the vegetables (carrot, onions, celery, leek) into very small dice (brunoise).

When the bones are nicely browned, add the vegetables. Cook for a further 15 minutes to caramelise them and extract as much juice as possible.

Add the flour, stir, and pour teverything into a large saucepan.

Place over a medium heat for 1 minute, stirring. Deglaze the juices from the oven dish by pouring in a small glass of water, scraping the bottom well, and then pour this into the saucepan.

Add 3 litres (6 pints 5 fl oz) of water, the tomato purée, garlic, bay leaves and thyme, then leave to cook at a low simmer for 3 hours.

Sieve through a conical strainer, discard the pieces and put the liquid into a saucepan over a medium heat. Bring to the boil and allow to reduce until you have a fairly dense, almost syrupy consistency. Allow to cool, overnight if possible, and skim the layer of fat off the surface.

To make the marrow in the red wine sauce, peel and finely slice the shallots, sweat them in the olive oil for 6–7 minutes over a medium heat until lightly coloured. Add the red wine and allow to reduce until there is almost no liquid left, but take care not to let it burn. Add 300 ml (10 fl oz) meat stock, scraping the bottom well. Allow to reduce again until you have a fairly dense, almost syrupy consistency. If there is any meat stock left, you can freeze it for later use.

Poach the marrow by immersing it in a pan of boiling salted water for 10 minutes. Drain, cool in iced water and cut into cubes. Add the marrow to the red wine sauce, season if necessary and add the wine vinegar. Serve straight away.

STARTERS

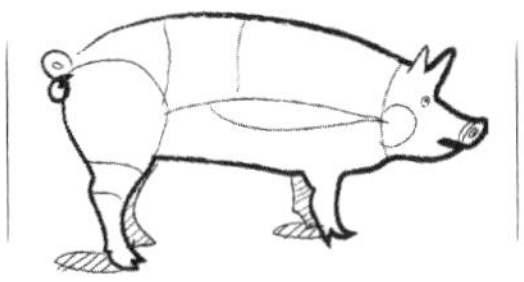

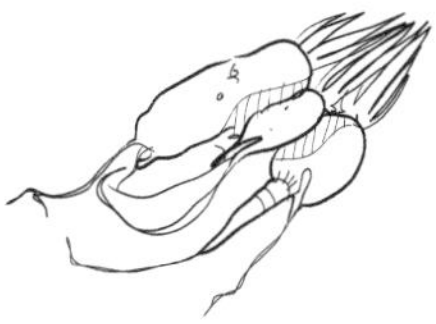

BEEF CARPACIO

Preparation 1 hour/ Cooking 20 minutes

SERVES 4

INGREDIENTS

320 g (11¼ oz) beef fillet
100 g (3½ oz) butter
2 extremely thin slices of sourdough bread
2 lemons
¼ bunch of chives
fleur de sel or similar sea salt (such as Maldon)
20 g (¾ oz) red miso paste
1 small fresh horseradish root
2 tablespoons olive oil

YOU WILL NEED
a brush

Preheat the oven to 150°C (300°F/Gas 2). Put the meat in the freezer for about 30 minutes; this makes it easier to slice.

In the meantime, clarify the butter by melting it gently; when it boils, skim the foam off the surface.

Brush the slices of bread with the clarified butter and put them in the oven on a baking tray for 20 minutes. Then cut them into small croutons.

Peel 1 lemon and remove the pith (exposing the pulp), remove the segments with a very sharp knife and cut them into small chunks.

Chop the chives.

Finely slice the meat (2 mm/⅛ in thick).

Arrange the slices on plates.

Sprinkle the meat with croutons, chives, a few chunks of lemon, a little fleur de sel, add a few dabs of red miso and grated horseradish, then drizzle with olive oil and a little lemon juice.

BEEF CHEEK TERRINE

with foie gras

Preparation 2 days + 1 hour / Cooking 5 hours 30 mins (approx.)

SERVES 4

INGREDIENTS

THE FOIE GRAS
1 small lobe fois gras (approx. 500 g/ 1 lb 2 oz), nerves removed by poulterer
1 tablespoon cognac
1 tablespoon ruby port
1 teaspoon salt
freshly ground black pepper

THE CHEEKS
3 beef cheeks (approx. 1.2 kg/2 lb 10 oz)
1 onion
1 carrot
2 garlic cloves
1 shallot
1 stick of celery
1 leek
a few sprigs of thyme
2 bay leaves
½ teaspoon coriander seeds
2 cloves
sea salt and freshly ground black pepper
6 sheets of gelatine (12 g/½ oz)

YOU WILL NEED
11.5 litre (3 pints 3 fl oz) terrine dish
casserole dish
whisk

The day before you want to serve this dish, season the entire surface of the foie gras with cognac, port, salt and pepper. Wrap in cling film (plastic wrap) and leave in the fridge to marinate for 24 hours. Also prepare the beef cheeks the day before: soak them in a large bowl of cold water for 24 hours in the fridge. Change the water several times until it is clear (there should be no blood or impurities).

Take the foie gras out of the fridge 1 hour before cooking. Remove the cling film (plastic wrap) and put it in the terrine dish, pack down well then pour on the marinade.

Place the terrine dish in a high-sided ovenproof dish to make a bain-marie. Pour boiling water into the oven dish three quarters of the way up the side of the terrine dish. Set the oven to 150°C (300°F/Gas 2) – no need to preheat – and place the foie gras inside. Allow to cook for about 40 minutes. If possible, check with a cook's thermometer: the temperature of the foie gras should not exceed 80°C (175°F). Take the terrine dish out of the oven, allow to cool, then place the foie gras on some cling film (plastic wrap) and roll it up tightly like a thick sausage. Put in the fridge to set for at least 6 hours.

To make the cheeks, peel the onion, carrot, garlic and shallot, and clean the celery and leek. Trim the cheeks of any excess fat and of the nerves with a good knife. Put the cheeks in a casserole dish, cover with cold water, bring to a boil then lower the heat. Skim any scum from the surface, add the vegetables, herbs and spices, then simmer over a low heat for 3–4 hours. The meat should be nice and tender. Remove the cheeks from the stock and allow to cool.

Strain the stock using a conical strainer and put it back on the stove to reduce at a low simmer until it is well concentrated. Remove from the heat and season to taste. Soak the gelatine in cold water. Drain when soft, then add it to the hot stock stirring with a whisk.

Cut the cheeks into 1 cm (½ in) cubes and season.

Form the terrine by putting a layer of the beef cheeks in the bottom of a terrine dish, then pour over some stock. Place the cylinder of foie gras in the middle of the dish on top of the cheeks. Put the rest of the cheek meat down the sides and on top of the fois gras. Pour over more stock to cover the cheeks. Leave to set for 24 hours. Arrange a slice of terrine with some Lentil Salad (page 252) on each plate.

Note: Resereve the remaining beef cheeks and stock and use in Beef Cheek Dumplings on page 78.

Grilled MARROW BONE

Preparation 2 days + 20 minutes / Cooking 10 minutes

SERVES 4

INGREDIENTS

4 marrow bones cut lengthwise
1 litre (34 fl oz) water
2 tablespoons spirit vinegar
ice cubes
fleur de sel (or Maldon salt)
coarsely ground pepper
1 bunch of chives

Soak the marrow bones in the cold water mixed with vinegar in the fridge, with ice cubes, for 48 hours.

Change the soaking water 3 or 4 times during this time until it is clear.

Drain the bones. Cook them on the barbecue or under a preheated grill for 10 minutes.

In a bowl, mix a little fleur de sel, pepper and freshly chopped chives. Sprinkle a little of this mixture on each marrow bone.

Serve the marrow bones with toast made from good country bread.

Marrow Bones stuffed with CHEEK AND FOIE GRAS

Preparation 1 day + 1 hour / Cooking 3 hours

SERVES 6

INGREDIENTS

- 2 beef cheeks
- 2 carrots
- 1 stick of celery
- 1 onion
- 3 tablespoons olive oil
- 2 garlic cloves
- 1 bouquet garni
- 200 ml (7 fl oz) beef stock (page 66)
- ½ litre full-bodied red wine such as Côtes-du-Rhône or Languedoc
- 6 marrow bones 8 cm (3 in) tall, nice and broad (ask your butcher for them)
- ½ bunch of chives
- ½ bunch of chervil
- 2 slices of foie gras weighing 100 g (3½ oz) each

The day before you wish to serve this dish, soak the beef cheeks in a large bowl filled with cold water for 24 hours.

Change the water several times until it is clear (there should be no more blood or impurities in it).

Chop the carrots, celery and onion into small dice of around 2 mm (⅛ in).

Sweat them in olive oil for a few minutes. Chop the garlic and add to the casserole dish to colour for about 1 minute.

Add the bouquet garni, the cheeks, the beef stock and wine. Cook on a very low heat for 3 hours. Add water if needed.

Meanwhile, blanch the marrow bones in simmering salted water for 8 minutes. Cool them in iced water. Take out the marrow and chill.

Put the empty bones back on the stove and cook in boiling water for 1 hour 30 minutes. This cleans them well and removes any impurities. Brush them clean.

When the cheeks are nice and tender, break them up with a fork in the casserole dish. Take out the bouquet garni and reduce the liquid as much as possible to obtain a nice thick texture. Chill until needed.

Once the cheeks are cooked, chop the herbs and cut the foie gras into dice. Add them to the stewed cheek. Reheat gently to combine the mixture.

Stuff the marrow bones with the beef cheek mixture and, just before serving, pop them in the oven for 10 minutes at 160°C (320°F/Gas 3). Serve with a salad accompaniment.

Note: The marrow can be used to make Beef Cheek Dumplings on page 78.

BEEF CHEEK

Dumplings

Preparation 2 day + 1 hour / Cooking 20 minutes

SERVES 4

INGREDIENTS

THE DUMPLINGS
1 large shallot
1 onion
1 garlic clove
sea salt and freshly ground black pepper
1 tablespoon olive oil
300 g (10½ oz) leftover beef cheek (or other beef) stock (page 72)
½ bunch of parsley
½ bunch of chives
flour, for dusting
8 sheets of Chinese dumpling pastry
1 egg yolk

THE BROTH
leftover stock vegetables, from beef cheek stock (page 72)
½ litre (17 fl oz) leftover beef stock (page 72)
a pinch of saffron threads
100 g (3½ oz) diced beef marrow (page 76)

YOU WILL NEED
a brush

First make the dumplings. Peel and finely slice the shallot, onion and garlic, then sweat in a frying pan with olive oil for 10 minutes over a medium to low heat.

Shred the beef cheeks, chop the herbs and mix with the onion, shallot and garlic. Season. Cover and leave this stuffing to rest in the fridge for 3 hours.

Sprinkle your worktop with flour. Place a sheet of dumpling pastry on it, put a little stuffing in the middle, brush the edges with egg yolk and stick a second sheet of pastry on top to close it. Get rid of as much air as possible around the stuffing so that the dumpling doesn't burst on cooking. Cut off any excess pastry around the stuffing, leaving a small margin around the edge to keep the stuffing in.

Repeat the same process for the other dumplings.

For the broth, cut the stock vegetables into dice and add them to the stock. Reheat then add the saffron and marrow and stir well.

Place one dumpling in each soup dish. Pour over the vegetable and marrow broth and serve hot.

RABBIT
Livers

Preparation 30 minutes / Cooking 40 minutes

SERVES 4

INGREDIENTS

THE LIVERS
300 g (10½ oz) rabbit livers
1 tablespoon grapeseed oil
15 g (½ oz) butter
100 g (3½ oz) smoked streaky bacon

THE GRIBICHE SAUCE
1 large egg
¼ bunch of tarragon
¼ bunch of chives
¼ bunch of parsley
¼ bunch of chervil
2 spring onions
3 small gherkins
1 tablespoon capers
1 tablespoon wholegrain mustard
3 tablespoons red wine vinegar
3 tablespoons olive oil
3 tablespoons grapeseed oil

MOUTARDE VIOLETTE SAUCE
3 tablespoons double (heavy) cream
1 tablespoon *moutarde violette* sauce (or any mild-flavoured mustard)

Remove any large nerves from the livers with a small knife.

Grill the livers on a barbecue or in a frying pan over a high heat in a little butter and oil for 1–2 minutes each side.

Cut the smoked streaky bacon into large dice and brown in a frying pan for 5 minutes until just crisp.

For the gribiche sauce, cook the egg for 9 minutes in a pan of boiling water. Finely chop the herbs, spring onions and gherkins and chop the egg. Mix together with the rest of the ingredients in a bowl.

For the moutarde violette sauce, mix the ingredients together in another bowl.

In each dish, arrange the livers with the cubes of streaky bacon, gribiche and *moutarde violette* sauce.

Serve with Lentil Salad (page 252).

PÂTÉ
EN CROÛTE

Preparation 1 day + 1 hr 30 mins / Cooking 2 hours 10 mins

MAKES ENOUGH FOR A 1.5 LITRE (3 PINTS 3 FL OZ) TERRINE

INGREDIENTS

THE PASTRY
1 kg (2 lb 3 oz) flour
350 g (12 oz) lard or butter (plus a little to grease the terrine dish)
300 g (10½ oz) warm water (over 60°C/140°F)
25 g (1 oz) salt
1 egg, beaten, for glazing

THE MAIN STUFFING
500 g (1 lb 2 oz) shoulder of veal
500 g (1 lb 2 oz) lean pork
500 g (1 lb 2 oz) pork jowl
2 garlic cloves
1 bunch of parsley
2 onions
1 shallot
250 ml (8½ fl oz) white wine
100 ml (3½ fl oz) red wine

THE CORE OF THE PÂTÉ
1 lobe fois gras (approx. 450 g 1 lb), nerves removed by poulterer
15 g (½ oz) salt
1 teaspoon pepper
2 tablespoons cognac
2 deboned saddles of rabbit
200 g (7 oz) *lardo di colonatta* (or other pork back fat)

THE FINE STUFFING
500 g (1 lb 2 oz) chicken breasts
4 egg whites
500 g (1 lb 2 oz) pouring cream

YOU WILL NEED
mincing machine
brush

Prepare the pastry, main stuffing and the core of the pâté the day before you want to serve this. For the pastry, put the flour in a food processor or large mixing bowl. Cut the lard into small cubes and rub into the flour using the food processor or your fingers to a breadcrumb consistency. Add the water and salt. Knead the pastry until it is nice and smooth. Wrap in cling film (plastic wrap) and chill in the fridge.

For the main stuffing, mince the shoulder of veal, lean pork and pork jowl, and put all the meat into a large bowl. Chop the garlic, parsley, onions and shallot, and add to the minced meats. Pour in the white and red wines then season. Mix everything together until well combined; cover the bowl and place in the fridge to marinate. For the pâté core, put the foie gras on to a piece of cling film (plastic wrap), season and drizzle with cognac. Roll the foie gras up tightly to form a sausage and put it in the fridge to marinate. Spread out the saddles of rabbit, season and roll them up into a sausage as well. Wrap the lardo di colonnata around the rolled-up rabbit. Cover in cling film (plastic wrap) and put in the fridge until needed.

On the day you are serving this dish start by making the fine stuffing. Cut the chicken breasts into large chunks and blend in a food processor with salt and pepper, gradually adding the cream then the egg whites. Preheat the oven to 180°C (350°F/Gas 4). Grease the terrine dish.

Roll out the pastry and cut out 2 rectangles long enough to line the sides of the terrine dish (each rectangle needs to cover one long and one short side and should stick out 1 cm (½ in) higher than the dish so the edges can be folded over the pastry lid), and one rectangle for the bottom. Line the terrine dish. Cut out a final rectangle for the lid.

Mix together the fine and main stuffing and put half of the mixture in the bottom of the terrine dish. Remove the cling film (plastic wrap) from the rabbit and bacon sausage, and from the foie gras sausage. Lay the rabbit on top of the stuffing mixture, then the foie gras on top of this. Spoon the rest of the stuffing around the sides and on top of the sausages. Put the pastry lid over the top of the pâté and fold over the edges sticking up from the pastry sides to keep the lid in place. You can use any leftover pastry to make a decoration of leaves or similar. Brush the beaten egg over the pastry as a glaze. Bake in the oven for 10 minutes then lower the temperature to 160°C (320°F/Gas 3). Put the terrine dish in a bain-marie and cook for a further 2 hours.

the
BEEF
CLUB
ENTRÉES
GALLOWAY
LONGHORN
SHORTHORN

GAZPACHO

Preparation 1 day + 45 minutes / Cooking 15 minutes /

SERVES 4

INGREDIENTS

4 large very ripe tomatoes
½ cucumber
1 red onion
2 garlic cloves
½ red pepper
4 drops of Tabasco (hot-pepper) sauce
1 slice of stale bread
1 tablespoon balsamic vinegar
1 tablespoon sherry vinegar
½ bunch of basil
6 tablespoons olive oil
1 tablespoon tomato purée (paste)
sea salt and freshly ground black pepper
12 ice cubes
12 salted anchovies, rinsed
1 foccacia (page 252) or 1 fine baguette, well toasted and drizzled with olive oil

The day before you want to serve this, immerse the tomatoes in boiling water for 1 minute, then peel and deseed them. Peel the cucumber, onion and garlic, and core and deseed the pepper. Cut all the vegetables into large cubes, but also cut some small cubes to garnish. Reserve the small cubes.

Place the large cubes of vegetables in a mixing bowl and add the Tabasco, stale bread, balsamic vinegar, sherry vinegar, basil (but retain some of the leaves for a garnish), 4 tablespoons of the olive oil and the tomato purée. Season, cover and put in the fridge until needed the next day.

Stir the gazpacho and adjust the seasoning if necessary. Keep chilled.

Serve the chilled gazpacho with the ice cubes, the small vegetable cubes, a few basil leaves, a little olive oil and the foccacia cut into rectangles and garnished with anchovies, if liked.

the
BEEF
CLUB
GALLOWAY
LONGHORN
SHORTHORN
HOMARD
BEEF BURGER

OCTOPUS
AND CHORIZO
kebabs

Preparation 15 minutes (if the octopus is cooked) / Cooking 5 minutes

SERVES 4

INGREDIENTS

2 teaspoons purée of *aji panca* (a South American chilli), alternatively use Espelette pepper paste or 1 spoonful of harissa mixed with 1 spoonful of tomato purée (paste)
2 tablespoons sweet soy sauce
a good pinch of cumin seeds
a small pinch salt
120 g (4 oz) chorizo
4 tentacles of an octopus cooked as in the recipe for Octopus Carpaccio (page 88)
2 tablespoons olive oil

Heat the grill or barbecue.

Mix the chilli purée, sweet soy sauce, cumin and salt. Finely slice the chorizo.

Cut the tentacles into approximately 2 cm (¾ in) pieces.

Thread the skewers alternately with pieces of octopus and chorizo.

Lightly brush the kebabs with olive oil and grill for about 5 minutes, turning several times and glazing with the chilli mixture while they are the cooking.

Serve on their own or with a small salad of crudités and a few parsley leaves.

OCTOPUS
CARPACCIO

Preparation 1 day + 30 minutes / Cooking 1 hour

SERVES 15
(not really worth doing for fewer people)

INGREDIENTS

1 octopus weighing 1.2–1.5 kg (2 lb 10–3 lb 5 oz)
a large pinch of powdered gelatine or agar-agar
1 quantity Mayonnaise Sauce with Olives (page 251)
2–3 tablespoons olive oil
20 g (¾ oz) Kalamata (black) olives, pitted
1 bunch of chives
1 orange

COURT BOUILLON
2 teaspoons coarse salt
1 onion
1 carrot
1 stick of celery
2 garlic cloves
100 ml (3½ fl oz) spirit vinegar
2 sprigs of thyme
2 bay leaves

To make the bouillon fill a large saucepan with water and the coarse salt. Add the onion, carrot, celery and garlic (washed and peeled), along with the vinegar, thyme and bay leaves. Bring to a boil. Immerse the octopus in the court bouillon, bring back to the boil then lower the heat and simmer gently for 45 minutes. Drain and allow to cool.

Cut off the tentacles and open and spread the body on a piece of cling film (plastic wrap). Arrange the tentacles on the body, sprinkle all over with powdered gelatine and roll up into a sausage. Wrap tightly. Put in the fridge to set for 24 hours.

Unwrap and finely slice the sausage and arrange the slices on individual plates or a serving dish. Criss-cross with sauce. Drizzle a little olive oil and orange juice on top, sprinkle with sliced olives, chopped chives and a little finely grated orange zest.

OYSTERS *and* BEEF

Preparation 5 minutes

SERVES 4

INGREDIENTS

24 oysters
100 g (3½ oz) *cecina* (a Spanish speciality of air-dried smoked beef), sliced very thinly (alternatively, substitute with air-dried beef such as *bindenfleisch*)
a few slices of lemon

Open the oysters. Keep the shell tops. Arrange on a dish alternating the oysters and empty shells (with the inside facing upwards).

Lay the slices of *cecina* in the shells.

Serve immediately with a few slices of lemon around them.

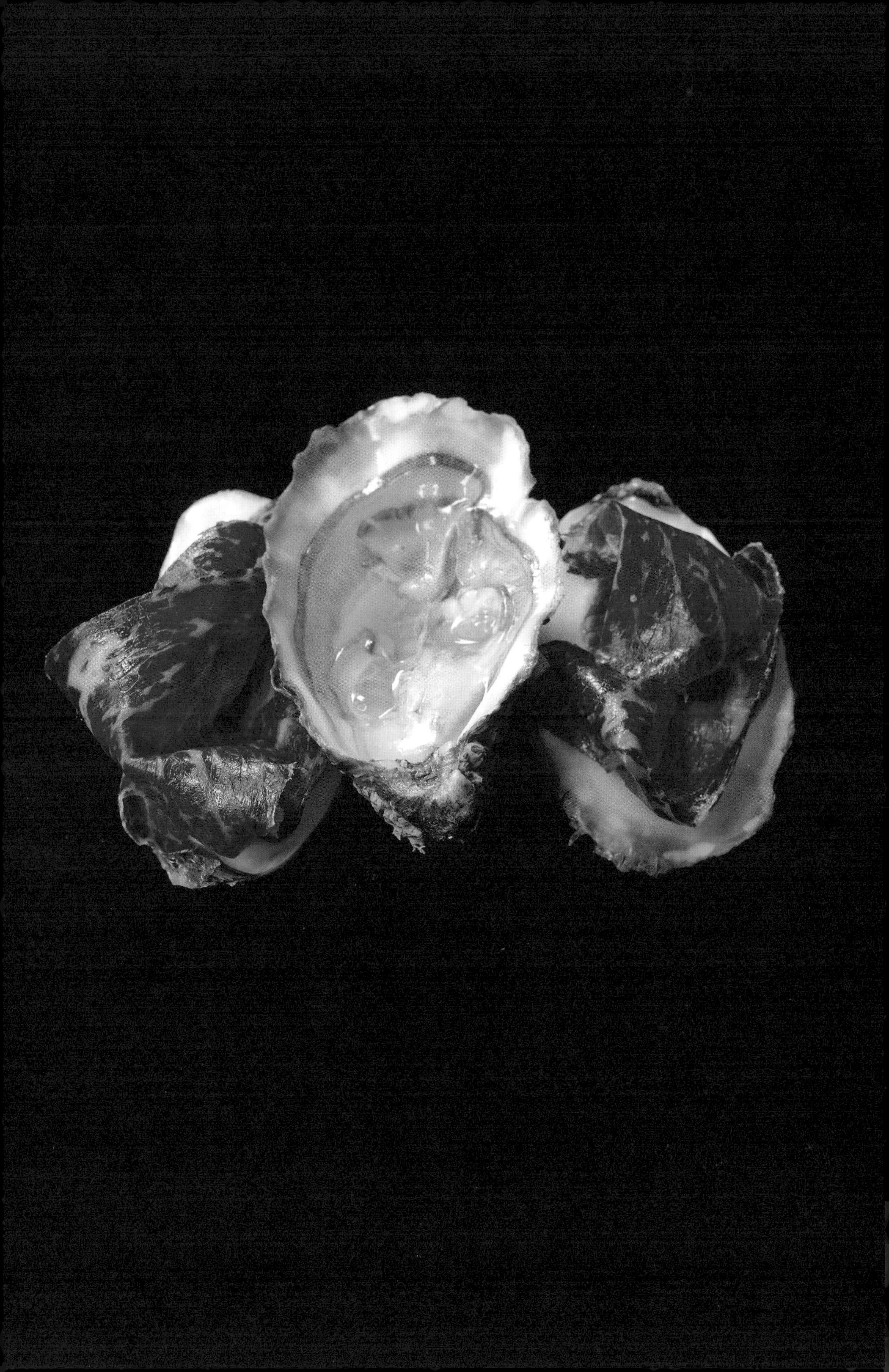

SEA BASS
CEVICHE

Preparation 50 minutes

SERVES 4

INGREDIENTS

300 g (10½ oz) coarse salt
60 g (2 oz) fine salt
500 g (1 lb 2 oz) skinless sea bass fillets
2 tablespoons salmon roe

THE MARINADE
4–5 limes
3 tablespoons olive oil
1 green (bell) pepper
1 red (bell) pepper
1 small red onion
¼ bunch of coriander
100 ml (3½ fl oz) Perrier (carbonated water)

Mix together the coarse and fine salts. Sprinkle half of it on a plate, lay the fillets on top and cover with the rest of the salt. Leave to rest for 15 minutes, then rinse the fillets with water and drain on kitchen paper.

Cut the fillets into approximately 1 cm (½ in) cubes.

To make the marinade, mix the juice and zest of 3–4 limes with the olive oil, very finely chopped peppers, very finely sliced onion, the chopped coriander and the Perrier.

Add the cubes of fish and marinade for 10 minutes, then stir.

Serve with the salmon roe and a slice of lime.

MAIN DISHES

SIRLOIN
TARTARE
with whisky

Preparation 20 minutes

SERVES 4

INGREDIENTS

800 g (1lb 12 oz) sirloin trimmed of gristle and fat (or, alternatively, a good rump steak)
50 ml (2 fl oz) olive oil
sea sealt and freshly ground black pepper

THE SAUCE
2 tablespoons capers
2 tablespoons small gherkins
2 spring onions (scallions)
2 tablespoons chives
1 tablespoon homemade mayonnaise
4 tablespoons ketchup
2 tablespoons wholegrain mustard
2 tablespoons peated whisky such as Laphroaig
1 tablespoon Worcestershire sauce
20 drops of Tabasco (hot-pepper) sauce

Cut the sirloin into cubes, no bigger than 1 cm (½ in).

For the sauce, chop the capers, gherkins, spring onions and chives. Tip into a bowl and mix in the rest of the ingredients.

Glaze the cubes of beef with olive oil, season and serve with the sauce.

MARINATED BEEF FILLET *with sesame seeds*

Preparation 1 day + 30 minutes / Cooking 5 minutes

SERVES 4

INGREDIENTS

300 g (10½ oz) beef fillet
400 g (14 oz) coarse salt
200 g (7 oz) sugar
1 tablespoon grapeseed oil

THE GARNISH
½ bunch of chives
1 tablespoon white sesame seeds
juice of 1 lemon
1 bundle of enoki mushrooms

THE SAUCE
1 tablespoon black sesame sauce (from Asian grocery stores)
4 tablespoons sesame oil

Put the fillet in a deep dish and cover with the sugar and salt mixed together. Cover with cling film (plastic wrap) and leave to marinate in a cold place for 24 hours. Rinse the fillet well and wipe dry with kitchen paper.

Fry the beef in the grapeseed oil for a few minutes over a high heat. The idea is to sear but not cook the meat; it should remain raw inside. Cover with cling film (plastic wrap) and put in the fridge for 2 hours.

In the meantime, mix the sauce ingredients together in a small bowl. Snip the chives.

When it is time to serve, cut very fine slices of fillet, drizzle with sauce, sprinkle with sesame seeds and chives, drizzle with lemon juice and accompany with the small raw mushrooms.

Anticuchos

HEART KEBABS

Preparation 12 hours + 20 minutes

FOR 12 KEBABS

INGREDIENTS

1 beef heart prepared by the butcher, cut into approx. 40 g (1½ oz) pieces

THE MARINADE

100 g (3½ oz) aji panca purée (from South American grocery stores) or alternatively 50 g (2 oz) harissa + 50 g (2 oz) tomato purée (paste)
1 tablespoon chopped garlic
2 tablespoons fresh oregano
4 tablespoons red wine vinegar
1 heaped teaspoon ground cumin
2 teaspoons salt
4 tablespoons grapeseed oil

YOU WILL NEED

skewers

Mix all the ingredients for the marinade together in a large bowl.

Put the pieces of heart in the marinade, cover with cling film (plastic wrap) and chill for 12 hours.

Make 12 kebabs and grill on the barbecue for 3 minutes each side to cook them medium rare.

The

BEEF BURGER

Preparation 1 hour / Cooking 40 minutes / Rest 2 hours 30 mins

SERVES 4

INGREDIENTS

¼ iceberg lettuce
4 tablespoons mayonnaise
2 tablespoons sweet relish (or alternatively, 4 large sweet and sour gherkins finely chopped)
1 red onion
4 buns (page 253)
8 slices of smoked streaky bacon
1 tablespoon grapeseed oil
4 minced beef patties weighing 150 g (5 oz) (with about 20% fat or marrow content)
4 slices (approx. 120 g/4 oz) Cheddar cheese (or similar)
Hamburger Sauce (page 250)

Preheat the oven to 180°C (350°F/Gas 4).

Finely slice the lettuce and mix with the mayonnaise and sweet relish. Peel and finely slice the onion.

Heat the rolls in the oven for 5 minutes. Fry the smoked streaky bacon in a frying pan for 7–8 minutes until nice and crispy.

Fry the minced beef patties for 1–2 minutes on each side in the oil over a medium–high heat. After turning the patties over, add the slices of onion around them to cook slightly.

Cut the rolls in half. Spread the bottom half with the lettuce mayonnaise, with a pattie top, slice of cheese, some onions, smoked bacon, and finish with the hamburger sauce (you may not need all of it). Close the bun and repeat with the other 3 rolls. Pop them into the oven for 2–3 minutes to reheat through.

Philly CHEESESTEAK

Preparation 30 minutes / Cooking 15 minutes

SERVES 3
(depending on their appetite)

INGREDIENTS

1–2 tablespoons grapeseed oil
450 g (1 lb) sirloin 3 mm (⅛ in) thick, with quite a lot of fat (or rib-eye)
3 buns (page 253), or 1 baguette cut into 3
Mayonnaise and Horseradish Sauce (page 252)
150 g (5 oz) provolone (from Italian delis, or other cheese that melts easily)
2 red onions, sliced
1 handful rocket (arugula)

THE SPICE MIX
3 tablespoons coriander seeds
3 tablespoons black peppercorns
50 g (2 oz) fine salt
45 g (1¾ oz) light brown sugar
30 g (1 oz) paprika
1 teaspoon ground ginger
1 teaspoon mace
3 garlic cloves
2 teaspoons strong mustard

Preheat the oven to 180°C (350°F/Gas 4).

First make the spice mix: spread the coriander seeds and peppercorns in a baking tray and put in the top of the oven for 5 minutes to toast (you can also do this in a hot dry frying pan).

In a spice grinder or pestle and mortar, blend the toasted coriander and pepper along with the salt, sugar, paprika, ground ginger and mace to a powder. Peel and, if necessary, de-germ (remove any sprouts that have started to grow from the cloves) the garlic. Purée the garlic in a garlic crusher or by finely grating it and add it to the dry spice mixture along with the mustard.

Add the oil to a griddle pan over a high heat and when the pan is very hot (the oil will start to smoke) put the sirloin in. Add the spice mixture to the pan according to your taste. Sear the meat for about 1 minute on each side; it should remain nice and juicy inside. Transfer the beef to a warm plate and leave to rest.

Preheat the grill. Cut the buns (or portions of baguette) in half, lay them on a grill pan and spread each slice with the mayonnaise and horseradish sauce. Grate the provolone and sprinkle it evenly over each piece of bread. Lay the sliced onions on the grill pan as well. Put under the grill for 1–2 minutes to melt the cheese and lightly cook the onion.

In the meantime, divide the sirloin into 3 pieces. Turn off the grill but keep the door closed to keep the oven hot. Assemble the burgers using a piece of sirloin and some onion and rocket inside each one. Put the burgers back in the hot oven for 1 minute to make the bread nice and crunchy.

BEEF *in* GUINNESS

Preparation 20 minutes / Cooking 3 hours 15 minutes

SERVES 4

INGREDIENTS

2 onions
1 tablespoon grapeseed oil
2 sprigs of thyme
3 bay leaves
4 garlic cloves, finely sliced
100 g (3½ oz) honey
1.2 kg (2 lb 10 oz) best rib of beef
500 ml (17 fl oz) beef stock (page 66)
1 litre (34 fl oz) Guinness
4 carrots, peeled and sliced
1 stick of celery, sliced
200 g (7 oz) salt pork belly, cut into lardons
a few sprigs of pea shoots

Preheat the oven to 160°C (320°F/Gas 3).

Finely slice the onions and sweat them in oil in a casserole dish for 6–7 minutes, with the thyme and bay leaves. Add the garlic and cook for a further 1–2 minutes. Add the honey, stir well and allow to caramelize (1–2 minutes).

Put the best ribs in the casserole dish, mix well to cover with the sauce and sear on all sides. Pour in the meat stock and Guiness and add the carrots, celery and pork belly. Put a lid on the dish and cook in the oven for 3 hours.

Remove the meat and set aside. Put the casserole dish on the hob to reduce the sauce until thick and almost syrupy. Return the meat to the casserole.

Serve with small sautéed potatoes. Sprinkle with pea shoots.

BEEF ROLLS

Preparation 20 minutes / Cooking 4 minutes

SERVES 4

INGREDIENTS

350 g (12 oz) skirt steak(or flank steak)
5–6 thin slices 2 mm (¼ in) thick, (approx. 80 g/3 oz total weight) of *lardo di colonnata* (pure pig fat), available from good Italian delis

Cut the meat against the grain in strips around 1.5 cm (¾ in) wide, 2 cm (¾ in) thick and 4 cm (1½ in) long.

Lay a piece of cling film (plastic wrap) on the work surface. Arrange the slices of *lardo di colonnata* on it side by side to make a long rectangle, allowing them to overlap slightly. Place the pieces of beef down the middle of the *lardo*. The idea is to roll the lardo up around a 'sausage' of beef, with the aid of the cling film (plastic wrap) which allows you to roll it up tightly. Cut the sausage into rolls of around 2 cm (¾ in) long.

Put a cocktail stick in each roll to stop it coming undone. Remove the cling film (plastic wrap).

Cook the beef rolls in a frying pan, without any extra fat, for 3–4 minutes over a high heat. They should be browned but the core should remain rare.

Classic MEATBALLS

Preparation 25 minutes / Cooking 20 minutes

SERVES 4

INGREDIENTS

THE MEATBALLS
1 onion
1 tablespoon olive oil
2 garlic cloves
½ bunch of parsley
500 g (1 lb 2 oz) minced (ground) beef
1 teaspoon fine salt
25 g (1 oz) breadcrumbs
a pinch of pepper
1 teaspoon ground star anise (or fennel)
1 large egg

THE SAUCE
1 large aubergine (eggplant)
2–3 tablespoons olive oil
3–4 garlic cloves unpeeled and crushed
2 sprigs of thyme
1 bay leaf
400 ml (13 fl oz) Tomato Sauce (page 251)
60 g (2 oz) Pecorino or Parmesan
½ bunch of marjoram or basil
a dash of olive oil

To make the meatballs, finely slice the onion and sweat in olive oil in a frying pan for 6–7 minutes. Finely slice the garlic and parsley. Stir together the onion, garlic and parsley with the remaining meatball ingredients. You can prepare this mixture the day before.

Preheat the oven to 200°C (400°F/Gas 6). With oiled hands shape the meatballs into the size of a ping pong ball. Put in an ovenproof dish and into the oven for 10 minutes.

To make the sauce cut the aubergine into large cubes and fry them in the olive oil over a medium–high heat for 5 minutes. Add the garlic cloves, thyme and bay leaf and cook for a further 5 minutes, until the aubergine is nicely golden and soft.

Put the meatballs with their cooking liquid into a saucepan and add the tomato sauce. Reheat gently.

Serve the meatballs in the sauce with cubes of aubergine, pecorino, a few marjoram or basil leaves and a dash of olive oil.

STAUB

Spicy MEATBALLS

Preparation 1 day + 35 minutes / Cooking 2 hours

SERVES 4

INGREDIENTS

THE BEANS
125 g (4 oz) black beans
½ red onion
1 garlic clove, peeled
½ tablespoon olive oil
500 ml (17 fl oz) chicken stock (or vegetable stock, or water)
a pinch of cumin or Triguisar seasoning (if you can find it)
a pinch of salt

THE MEATBALLS
1 onion
1 tablespoon olive oil
2 garlic cloves
½ bunch of summer savory
500 g (1 lb 2 oz) minced beef
10 g (½ oz) fine salt
25 g (1 oz) breadcrumbs
1 large egg
1 teaspoon ground cumin
1 teaspoon ground coriander
1 teaspoon hot pepper sauce
1 teaspoon ground anise

THE GARNISH
40 g (1½ oz) double cream
½ bunch of dill
60 g (2 oz) Cheddar
1 green (bell) pepper
1 red (bell) pepper
½ bunch of coriander (cilantro)
½ red onion

Prepare the beans the day before you want to make this dish. Put the beans in a large bowl and fill with cold water so that there is at least 5 cm (2 in) water covering them. Leave the beans to soak overnight; this reduces the amount of time you will need to cook the beans for and helps ensure they will be tender.

Drain the beans and set aside. Finely slice the red onion and purée the garlic using a garlic crusher or by finely grating it. Add the oil to a large deep saucepan or stockpot over a medium heat and sweat the onions for 6–7 minutes. Add the garlic, beans, chicken stock and cumin, and bring to the boil. Reduce the heat and simmer gently for 1–1½ hours, or until the beans are tender. Add a pinch of salt halfway through. Depending on the age of the beans they can take longer to cook, so check them regularly and continue cooking for more time if needed. Add more water if the pan starts to dry out.
The beans should absorb a large amount of liquid, so only drain them if necessary after they have cooked.

While the beans are cooking, make the meatballs. Finely slice the onion and sweat in the olive oil in a frying pan for 6–7 minutes. Finely chop the garlic and summer savory. In a large bowl, mix together the onion, garlic and savory with the remaining meatball ingredients until everything is well combined. You can prepare this mixture the day before and keep it covered in the fridge if you prefer.

Preheat the oven to 200°C (400°F/Gas 6). Shape the meat mixture into ping pong balls with oiled hands. Put them in an ovenproof dish and cook in the oven for 10 minutes. Remove and leave to rest for 15 minutes, then transfer the meatballs with their cooking liquid into the pot of cooked beans and stir through. If the beans or meatballs have been allowed to cool down before you are ready to serve, reheat them over a gentle heat. Serve them in a large dish, drizzle with some cream, snip over some dill and sprinkle with grated Cheddar. Garnish with a little mix of diced peppers, coriander and onion.

STAUB
STAUB

UDDERS
TONGUE
and Tripe

Preparation 1 hour + 50 minutes / Cooking 4 hours 10 minutes

SERVES 4

INGREDIENTS

300 g (10½ oz) tongue
300 g (10½ oz) udders
300 g (10½ oz) tripe
2 tablespoons grapeseed oil

THE STOCK
2 garlic cloves
1 onion
1 carrot
1 stick of celery
1 tablespoon coarse sea salt
2 sprigs of thyme
2 bay leaves

THE SEASONING
3 tablespoons grapeseed oil
1 tablespoon sherry vinegar
sea salt and freshly ground black pepper
1 green (bell) pepper, diced
1 red (bell) pepper, diced
1 red onion, diced
a few basil leaves

YOU WILL NEED
a brush

Make a stock by putting the garlic, onion, carrot and celery (washed and peeled as necessary) with the salt, thyme and bay leaves into a large cooking pot of salted water. Add the pieces of meat. Bring to the boil then reduce the heat to a simmer, with the lid on. After about 2 hours, remove the udders, then after 3 hours, the tongue. After 4 hours, the tripe should also be cooked. Check each piece of meat before removing it: the meat should be tender and yield to the point of a knife. Once all the meat is done, put everything back into the cooking pot and leave to cool in the stock.

Prepare the barbecue.

Slice the teats, tongue and tripe, and brush with a little oil. Grill on the barbecue, just long enough to turn the pieces golden brown. They can also be browned in the frying pan.

Dress with oil, vinegar, a little salt and pepper, and garnish with the chopped peppers and onion, and a few young basil leaves.

BEEF
CLUB
HOMARD
LANGOUSTINE
PLATS

PORK BELLY
At The Beef Club

CALF
Sweetbreads

Preparation 2 days + 30 minutes / Cooking 25 minutes

SERVES 4

INGREDIENTS

4 calf sweetbreads (160 g/5½ oz each)
150 ml (5 fl oz) beef stock (page 66) or veal stock
1 tablespoon grapeseed oil
15 g (½ oz) butter
sea salt and freshly ground black pepper

THE VEGETABLES
4 young carrots with leaves on
½ yellow beetroot (beet)
½ Chioggia beetroot (beet)
2 small red beetroots (red beets)
1 parsnip
4 small turnips with leaves on
4–5 spring onions (scallions)
4 green asparagus spears
2 tablespoons olive oil
15 g (½ oz) butter
fleur de sel

THE GREMOLATA
2 tablespoons sunflower seeds
1 orange
½ bunch of coriander(cilantro)
sea salt and freshly ground black pepper
3 tablespoons olive oil

Leave the calf sweetbreads to soak in cold water 48 hours in advance. Change the water several times a day; it should be clear at the end.

Prepare the vegetables. Carefully wash and peel, if necessary, the carrots, beetroots, parsnip, turnips and onions, and cut the woody base off the asparagus spears. Cut the vegetables into chunks or batons, depending on their shape, of matching sizes. Keep the base of the leaves on the carrots and turnips.

Cook each different vegetable separately by immersing them successively in boiling salted water for approximately 2–4 minutes, keeping them nice and firm. Each time, immerse the vegetables in iced water after draining, to halt the cooking process. Just before serving, brown all the vegetables in olive oil and butter for 2–3 minutes in a large sauté pan over a medium–high heat. Sprinkle with fleur de sel.

Toast the sunflower seeds in a hot, dry frying pan, stirring constantly until slightly browned.

Peel and segment the orange, removing the pith and inner skins. Cut the segments into small pieces. Chop the coriander and mix it with the sunflower seeds, salt and pepper. Thin out the mixture with a little oil, then add the orange pieces.

Take the calf sweetbreads out of the soaking water and cook in boiling salted water for 10 minutes. Drain, then immerse in iced water to cool.

Fry the drained calf sweetbreads in the oil and butter over a fairly high heat just long enough to turn them golden (1–2 minutes each side).

Add the beef stock, season and allow to reduce for 3–4 minutes.

Serve the sweetbreads with their sauce, the vegetables, and the gremolata on top.

Pork BELLY

Preparation 1 day + 35 minutes / Cooking 1 hour 30 mins

SERVES 4

INGREDIENTS

2 Granny Smith apples
2 onions
½ head of celery
1 kg (2 lb 3 oz) fresh pork belly
330 ml (11 fl oz) wheat beer
1 teaspoon cumin seeds
3 garlic cloves, finely chopped
1 teaspoon coriander seeds
3–4 sprigs of thyme
2 bay leaves
homemade Smoky Sauce (page 250)

Peel and dice the apples and onions. Chop the celery.

Put the pork belly in a large bowl to marinate with the beer, apples, celery and onions. Add the cumin seeds, chopped garlic, coriander, thyme and bay leaves. Mix well, cover and leave to rest in a cold place for a day.

Put everything into a stewpot and simmer very gently for approximately 1 hour, until the belly is very tender. Allow to cool.

Cut thick slices of the pork belly and sear quickly in a frying pan over a high heat to brown them.

Pour the smoky sauce into the frying pan with the pork, scrape the bottom of the frying pan with a wooden spoon and turn the slices over to coat well with sauce. Lower the heat and cook for a further 10 minutes. Serve.

HOMEMADE SAUSAGE

Preparation 2 hours / Cooking 15 minutes

MAKES 10 THICK SAUSAGES

INGREDIENTS

2 garlic cloves
1 kg (2 lb 3 oz) fresh pork belly without rind or cartilage
1 kg (2lb 3 oz) deboned pork spare rib
2 white onions
200 g (7 oz) dry-cured slab bacon (unsmoked)
30 g (1 oz) salt
1 teaspoon pepper
a good pinch of strong cayenne pepper
40 g (1½ oz) breadcrumbs
2 metres (6 ft 7 in) pork casings (from the pork butcher)
20 g (¾ oz) butter
1 teaspoon olive oil

YOU WILL NEED
meat mincer
sausage funnel

Peel and roughly chop the garlic. Pass the fresh pork belly and the deboned pork spare rib through the meat mincer, using plate size 8, inserting the garlic and onions.

Cut the bacon into small dice. Mix the salt, pepper and cayenne pepper in half a glass of water.

Mix together the minced meat and breadcrumbs, bacon and diluted seasoning. Leave this mixture to rest in the fridge for 1 hour.

Insert the stuffing into the pork casing with the aid of the funnel, then cut into 10 sausages.

They will keep for a week in the fridge.

Just before serving, fry the sausages in butter with a little olive oil. Serve with Mashed Potato (page 142).

SCOTCH EGGS

Preparation 1 day + 55 minutes / Cooking 15 minutes

SERVES 4

INGREDIENTS

4 fresh organic eggs
vegetable oil, for frying
mixed young salad
grilled smoked streaky bacon

THE STUFFING
2 Toulouse sausages (200–250 g/7–9 oz)
2 Montbéliard sausages (200–250 g /7–9 oz)
50 g (2 oz) chicken livers
1 shallot
½ bunch of parsley
75 ml (2½ fl oz) white wine
white pepper
1 garlic clove

THE COATING
50 g (2 oz) plain (all-purpose) flour
1 large egg, beaten
100 g (3½ oz) Japanese Panko breadcrumbs (or ordinary dry breadcrumbs)

YOU WILL NEED
meat mincer

Prepare the stuffing the day before you want to serve this. Take the sausages out of their skins and mix the meat together with all the stuffing ingredients. Pass the mixture through the meat mincer or chop finely with a knife. Leave to rest in the fridge for 24 hours; this helps the flavours to develop.

On the day, cook the eggs in boiling water for 6 minutes until soft-boiled. Cool in iced water and gently remove the shells. Take a heaped spoonful of stuffing and coat each egg with it taking care not to break it. Set the eggs aside in the freezer for 30 minutes to harden.

Heat the oil in a deep fat fryer to 170°C (340°F). Roll each egg in the flour, the beaten egg then the breadcrumbs. Fry them one by one for 6–7 minutes until nicely browned all over.

Serve immediately with mixed young salad leaves garnished with grilled smoked streaky bacon. If you are not serving the eggs immediately, put them in a hot oven (180°C/350°F/Gas 4) for 5 minutes just before serving.

18/03
18/03
18/03
18/03
18/03

BEEF CLUB
The Terrace

Grilled LOBSTER

Preparation 20 minutes / Cooking 10 minutes

SERVES 4

INGREDIENTS

2 Breton lobsters 600–800 g (1 lb 5 oz–1lb 12 oz) each
100 ml (3½ fl oz) olive oil
salt
a pinch of Espelette pepper
100 ml (3½ fl oz) absinthe

Separate the claws from the bodies of the lobster by making a quarter turn to release them.

Bring 2 large saucepans of salted water to the boil.

Cook the claws for 3 minutes and the bodies for 2 minutes. Cool in iced water.

Cut the lobster bodies in half lengthways with a knife, remove the creamy parts, coral and intestines.

Crack open the claws and segments (with a hammer or nutcracker), then place the split claws, with the meat exposed, in the heads.

Drizzle the lobsters-halves with a little olive oil and sprinkle with Espelette pepper and salt.

Put under a very hot grill or on the barbecue for 5–6 minutes. The lobsters must be cooked by a very high heat source because they must cook quickly so as not to dry out.

To serve, heat the absinthe in a small saucepan, set light to it and pour it over the lobsters. The half-lobsters can be served as surf and turf alongside pieces of meat.

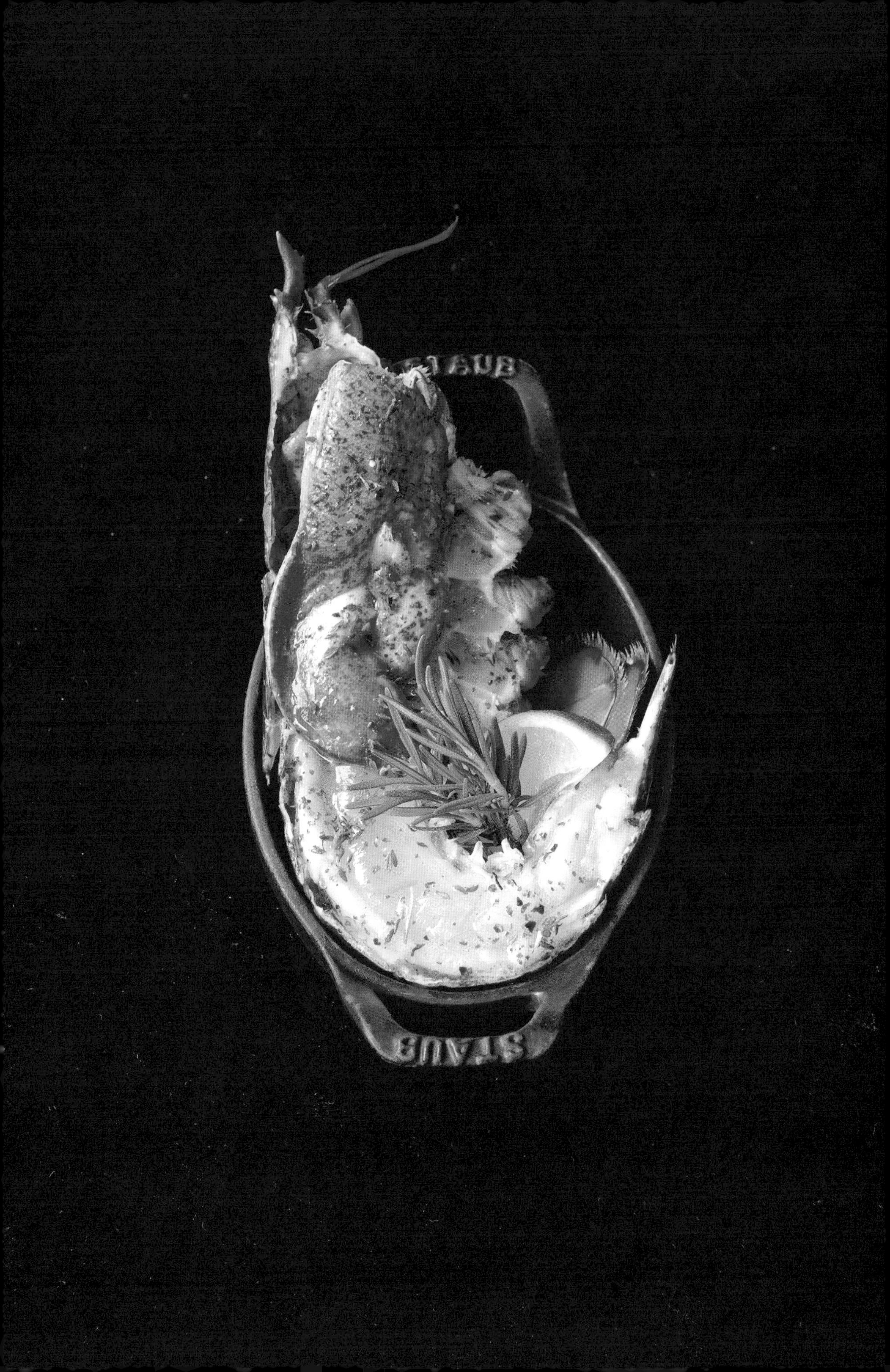
STAUB

Breton LANGOUSTINES

Preparation 30 minutes / Cooking 5 minutes

SERVES 4

INGREDIENTS

THE LANGOUSTINES
20 langoustines
2 eggs
100 g (3½ oz) Japanese Panko breadcrumbs (or ordinary dry breadcrumbs)
vegetable oil, for frying
1 lime

THE REMOULADE
1 head of celery with leaves
100 g (3½ oz) crab meat
¼ celeriac, grated
1 tablespoon mayonnaise
1 teaspoon white balsamic vinegar (or traditional balsamic vinegar, but well sweetened)
a few drops of Tabasco (hot-pepper sauce)
a good pinch of sweet paprika
sea salt and freshly ground black pepper

Remove the heads of the langoustines and take away the shell, but keep the last 2 rings and the tail. Take out the gut.

Separate the whites from the egg yolks, keep the yolks for another recipe. Prepare 2 dishes for the breadcrumb coating: the beaten egg whites in one, the breadcrumbs in the other.

Dip each langoustine in the egg white then in the breadcrumbs, set aside on a dish.

Cut the celery into small 2 mm (⅛ in) dice and snip the leaves. Mix the crab, celeriac, mayonnaise, vinegar, Tabasco and paprika, then season well.

Heat the oil in a saucepan or frying pan, to 170–180°C (340–350°F). Fry the langoustines for 2–3 minutes.

When ready to serve, grate a little lime zest on to the fried langoustines and serve with the remoulade. Place a segment of lime, peel and pith removed, on top of the remoulade.

CUTTLEFISH *with* FENNEL

Preparation 30 minutes / Cooking 15 minutes

SERVES 4

INGREDIENTS

THE CUTTLEFISH
600 g (1 lb 5 oz) cuttlefish fillets
1 tablespoon olive oil
1 garlic clove
½ bunch of parsley
a pinch of saffron threads

THE FENNEL
3 fennel bulbs
olive oil
1 teaspoon fennel seeds
100 ml (3½ fl oz) water
salt
juice of ½ a lemon

THE TOMATOES AND GARNISH
40 g (1½ oz) Taggiasche olives (or Kalamata olives)
10 Dried Tomatoes (page 253) or shop-bought sundried tomatoes
grated zest of 1 orange
sea salt and freshly ground black pepper
2 teaspoons olive oil

YOU WILL NEED
ice cubes
a mandoline

Cut 2 of the fennel bulbs into quarters.

Brown them on all sides in the olive oil for 2–3 minutes in a frying pan over a fairly high heat. Add the fennel seeds, stir, add the water, a little salt, and cook over a low heat until the bulbs are nice and soft (7–8 minutes). Drizzle a little lemon juice over the fennel and set aside.

Cut the fresh tomatoes into quarters and pit and slice the olives. Cut the remaining fennel bulb into very thin slices and put them in a bowl of water with some ice cubes.

Score the outside of the cuttlefish in a criss-cross pattern and sauté it in the olive oil for 2 minutes over a high heat. Add the finely sliced garlic, the parsley leaves (keep a few for garnish) and the saffron threads. Stir and remove from the heat.

Serve the cuttlefish with the cooked fennel, dried tomatoes, olives, the orange zest and the raw fennel drained and drizzled with a little olive oil. Season, drizzle with a few drops of olive oil and sprinkle with the remaining parsley.

CLAMS
in Champagne

Preparation 2 day + 25 minutes / Cooking 20 minutes

SERVES 4

INGREDIENTS

THE CLAMS
1.2 kg (2 lb 10 oz) clams
2 shallots
15 g (½ oz) butter
3 tablespoons Parsley Butter (page 250)
1 tablespoon crème fraîche
1 glass of Champagne

THE CRISPY BREADCRUMBS
100 g (3½ oz) smoked streaky bacon
60 g (2 oz) breadcrumbs
1–2 spring onions (scallions)

Two days before you make this dish, soak the clams in a large basin of water. Change the water 5–6 times during the 48 hours to remove any sand.

Cut the smoked streaky bacon into fine lardons. Fry in a frying pan for about 5 minutes, then add the breadcrumbs and stir well for 1–2 minutes to coat with fat and grill lightly. Slice the spring onions very finely.

Finely slice and sweat the shallots in the butter in a large saucepan over a medium to gentle heat for 6 –7 minutes until soft and transparent.

Add the clams, parsley butter and the crème fraîche. Put on the lid and turn the heat up to high (without lifting the lid) to open the clams. Remove the lid and add the Champagne.

Stir well and serve immediately with the crispy breadcrumbs and a few slices of spring onion.

CRAB

Cakes

Preparation 1 hour + 70 minutes / Cooking 20 minutes

SERVES 6

INGREDIENTS

THE STUFFING
2 shallots
1 tablespoon grapeseed oil
1 bunch of basil
1 piece of ginger (4 cm/1½ in)
½ kaffir lime (or ½ lime)
500 g (1 lb 2 oz) crab meat
100 g (3½ oz) mayonnaise
4 egg yolks
1 large pinch of Espelette pepper
1 teaspoon Old Bay Seasoning (American spice mix, can be substituted with a pinch of *quatre épices* + a pinch of paprika + 1 bay leaf ground)
sea salt and freshly ground black pepper

THE BREADCRUMBS
1 egg yolk
100 g (3½ oz) plain (all-purpose) flour
100 g (3½ oz) Japanese Panko breadcrumbs (or ordinary breadcrumbs)
vegetable oil, for frying

TO SERVE
Spicy Mayonnaise (page 251)

For the stuffing, finely slice the shallots and sweat in oil in a frying pan for 5–6 minutes. Chop the basil, grate the ginger and the zest of the lime. Transfer to a bowl with the shellfish and carefully mix together with the rest of the ingredients for the stuffing and season. Form the mixture into a sausage 2–3 cm (¾–¼ in) in diameter and wrap in cling film (plastic wrap). Put it in the freezer for 30–40 minutes to set.

Heat the frying oil to 180°C (350°F) in a wide, high saucepan or a deep-fat fryer.

Take the stuffing out of the freezer and cut into pieces of approximately 2 cm (¾ in) . Roll each piece in the beaten egg yolk, then in the flour and finally in the breadcrumbs. Fry the crab cakes in batches – turning once, about 2 minutes each side, they should be a nice golden colour. Drain on kitchen paper.

Serve with the spicy mayonnaise and a little salad of crudités. If you are not serving them straight away, you can reheat them for 5–10 minutes in the oven at 150°C (302°F/Gas 2).

SIDE DISHES

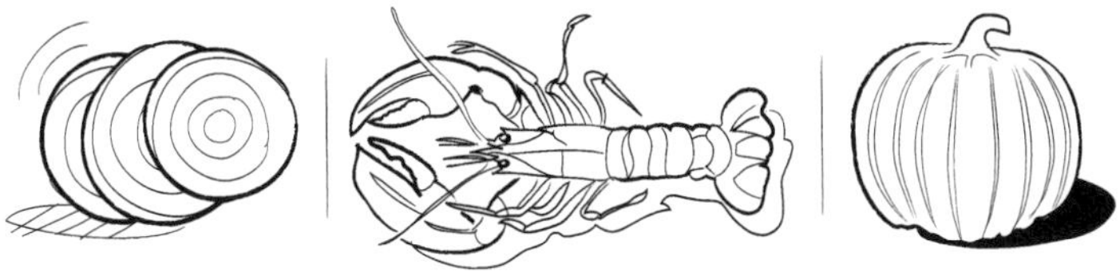

POTATO
WEDGES

Preparation 10 minutes / Cooking 25 minutes

SERVES 4

INGREDIENTS

1 kg (2 lb 3 oz) Charlotte potatoes
1 litre (34 fl oz) duck fat
vegetable oil, for frying
fine salt

Wash the potatoes and cut into large wedges leaving the skins on. Rinse them in water twice to remove excess starch and dry with a clean tea towel.

Melt the duck fat in a large saucepan and heat to 130°C (265°F). Cook the potato wedges gently for around 20 minutes without letting them colour. They should be cooked through. Drain.

Heat the oil in a deep pan or deep-fat fryer to 180°C (350°F) and, just before serving, and immerse the potatoes for 5–7 minutes to brown them and make them nice and crisp. Drain and season with salt.

RATTE MASHED *Potato*

Preparation 20 minutes / Cooking 45 minutes

SERVES 4

INGREDIENTS

1 kg (2 lb 3 oz) large ratte potatoes, or other waxy white potatoes
500 ml (17 fl oz) milk
300 g (10 ½ oz) butter
salt

YOU WILL NEED
potato ricer or mouli

Boil the potatoes in a large pan of salted water for 35–45 minutes until soft.

Peel the potatoes while still warm, then press through the potato ricer, using the fine disc.

Heat the milk in a saucepan and cut the butter into chunks.

Work the butter into the mash with a spatula, gradually incorporating the milk. Season with salt.

MAC *and* CHEESE

Preparation 25 minutes / Cooking 30 minutes

SERVES 6

INGREDIENTS

150 g (5 oz) Stilton (or other blue cheese)
150 g (5 oz) cheddar (or other melting cheese) cut into chunks
150 g (5 oz) unpasteurised farm raclette cheese
1 litre (34 fl oz) béchamel sauce (page 250)
600 g (1 lb 5 oz) macaroni (or conchiglie)
salt
1 garlic clove
100 g (3½ oz) Cheddar (or other melting cheese) grated
2–3 tablespoons breadcrumbs

Gently melt together the Stilton, the chunks of Cheddar and raclette into the béchamel sauce over a low heat. Stir well to prevent the cheese from sticking to the bottom.

Cook the pasta to al dente in a large saucepan of salted boiling water, then drain and leave to cool.

Rub an ovenproof dish with the garlic clove cut in half. Mix the pasta and cheese béchamel sauce, pour into the dish and sprinkle with the grated cheddar and breadcrumbs. Put in a hot oven for 10 minutes.

HOMARD BRETON ENTIER
ACCOMPAGNEMENTS
FRITES MAISON
pommes de terre Charlotte cuites à la graisse de canard
MAC AND CHEESE
conchiglie rigate gratinées aux fromages :
stilton, montgomery cheddar & ogleshield
ENDIVE, TRÉVISE, CRESSON & NOIX
vinaigrette au raisiné
montgomery cheddar & vinaigrette au miel
10€
caramelisées à la cannelle
10€

CANNELLONI

Gratin

Preparation 50 minutes / Cooking 45 minutes

SERVES 4

INGREDIENTS

8 cannelloni
salt
400 ml (13 fl oz) homemade tomato sauce (page 251)
60 g (2 oz) Cheddar (or other melting cheese)

THE STUFFING
1 brocciu cheese
1 large egg
½ bunch of mint, leaves taken off and chopped, plus extra sprigs to garnish
salt, pepper

YOU WILL NEED
ice cubes
piping bag

Cook the cannelloni in a large saucepan of salted water, then cool in iced water.

Mix all the stuffing ingredients together. Stuff the cannelloni using a piping bag (or a small spoon), then lay them in a dish. Cover with sauce, then grated Cheddar.

Put under the grill for 15 minutes to brown the top. Garnish with sprigs of mint and serve.

STAUB
STAUB

Vegetable CASSOLETTE

Preparation 40 minutes / Cooking 10 minutes

SERVES 4

INGREDIENTS

4 young carrots
1 yellow beetroot (beet)
1 Chioggia beetroot (beet)
1 parsnip
4–5 spring onions (scallions)
1 swede
½ black radish
½ head of broccoli
½ cauliflower
1 handful of broad beans (fava beans), unshelled
500 g (1 lb 2 oz) peas (unshelled weight)
1 handful of green beans
12 mini leeks
2 tablespoons olive oil
15 g (½ oz) butter
fleur de sel

Carefully wash and peel the carrots, beetroots, parsnip, spring onions, swede and black radish. Wash the broccoli and cauliflower and separate into florettes. Shell the broad beans and peas. Trim the green beans. Wash the leeks, remove the roots and any hard parts. Cut the vegetables into chunks or batons in matching sizes. Slice the spring onions fairly thickly.

Cook each different vegetable separately in boiling salted water for about 4 minutes, to keep them nice and firm. Each time immerse them in iced water straight after cooking and draining to halt the cooking process. For the green vegetables, use iced salted water to keep their green colour.

When serving, brown all the vegetables for 2–3 minutes in olive oil and butter in a large sauté pan, over a fairly high heat, beginning with the root vegetables and finishing with the green vegetables. Do this in batches if necessary. Sprinkle with fleur de sel and arrange attractively.

STAUB
STAUB

GRILLED TOMATOES *and Peppers*

Preparation 1 day +1 hour / Cooking 30 minutes

SERVES 4

INGREDIENTS

THE PEPPERS
2 red (bell) peppers
100 ml (3½ fl oz) olive oil
2 sprigs of thyme
2 garlic cloves, finely sliced

THE TOMATOES
4 large ripe tomatoes (or 8 small ones)
6 tablespoons red wine vinegar
100 ml (3½ fl oz) olive oil
2 green tomatoes
1 white onion, finely chopped
½ bunch of parsley, chopped
Espelette pepper

The day before you want to make this dish, roast the red peppers on the barbecue or in the oven preheated to 200°C (400°F/Gas 6) for 20–30 minutes, turning regularly to grill the skin on all sides. Put in a bowl and cover with a lid or with cling film (plastic wrap).

After a few minutes, the skin will come off easily. Peel then slice and remove the seeds and the white parts from inside the peppers. Put the peppers to marinate overnight in the oil, thyme and garlic.

On the day, remove the stalks from the tomatoes and cut into quarters. Put them in a bowl in the vinegar and olive oil, and add the finely minced onion. Marinate for 1 hour.

Serve the strips of pepper with the marinated tomatoes, parsley and a little Espelette pepper.

Add the green tomatoes, sliced and keep chilled until ready to serve.

Mushrooms in PARSLEY

Preparation 20 minutes / Cooking 10 minutes

SERVES 4

INGREDIENTS

1 kg (2 lb 3 oz) medium-sized white mushrooms
3 tablespoons olive oil
4 tablespoons Parsley Butter (page 250)
sea salt and freshly ground black pepper

Wash the mushrooms under a running tap briefly and remove the stems. (You can keep the stems to add to a stock.) Fry the mushrooms in olive oil for a few minutes to brown slightly, then season.

Add the parsley butter to the frying pan and toss the mushrooms in it to coat well. Season again if necessary (taste first as the butter is salted) and serve.

STAUB
the BEEF CLUB
POISSONS
HOMARD
LANGOUSTINE
GALLOWAY
RUMSTECK
maison au whisky · servi avec un accompagnement au choix

STEAMED SPINACH

Preparation 10 minutes / Cooking 5 minutes

SERVES 4

INGREDIENTS

600 g (1 lb 5 oz) fresh spinach leaves
150 ml (5 fl oz) olive oil
fleur de sel
1 bulb barlic (optional)

Wash the spinach by immersing the leaves in water to remove any dirt. If the leaves are really large, remove the stems. Drain well.

Heat a little oil in a frying pan and wilt the spinach in small quantities. Drizzle with olive oil using a spoon. Sprinkle with a little fleur de sel and serve.

You can keep a few attractive raw young spinach leaves for a garnish or decorate the dish with an oven-roasted garlic bulb.

STAUB
STAUB

SWISS CHARD *and marjoram* GRATIN

Preparation 30 minutes / Cooking 35 minutes

SERVES 4

INGREDIENTS

1 bunch Swiss chard
6 tablespoons olive oil
60 g (2 oz) butter
100 ml (3½ fl oz) water
1 litre (34 fl oz) Béchamel Sauce (page 250)
2 garlic cloves
½ bunch marjoram
80 g (3 oz) pecorino or Parmesan
a pinch of red pepper flakes

Separate the white parts of the Swiss chard from the green. Peel the whites, if necessary, by removing the fibre that forms a kind of skin. Cut into cubes.

Sauté the greens quickly in 3 tablespoons of olive oil and set aside. Sauté the whites in the remaining oil and the butter. Add the water and allow to cook for 10 minutes until nice and soft.

Preheat the oven to 190°C (375°F/Gas 5).

In an ovenproof dish, mix together the greens, whites and béchamel sauce. Chop and add the garlic and marjoram, then sprinkle with grated or shaved pecorino cheese grated or in flakes. Bake in the oven for 15 minutes. Sprinkle with the red pepper flakes and serve.

the BEEF CLUB
ENTRÉES
PALOURDES & CHAMPAGN
cuites au four, ail & persil
ENTRECÔTE
FAUX-FILET
RUMSTECK
STAUB

PUMPKIN *and* MOZZARELLA

Preparation 15 minutes / Cooking 45 minutes

SERVES 4

INGREDIENTS

¼ pumpkin
100 ml (3½ fl oz) olive oil
sea salt and freshly ground black pepper
1 garlic clove
1 sprig thyme
1 bay leaf
30 g (1 oz) pumpkin seeds
¼ bunch of watercress (or other mixed leaves)
2 balls of mozzarella (125 g/4 oz each)
1 teaspoon curry powder

THE VINAIGRETTE
juice of 1 orange
juice of ½ lemon
6 tablespoons olive oil
sea salt and freshly ground black pepper

Preheat the oven to 180°C (350°F/ Gas 4). Peel the pumpkin, cut into 4, lay the pieces in an ovenproof dish and season with olive oil, salt and pepper. Crush the garlic in its skin and add it along with the thyme leaves and bay leaf. Roast in the oven until the pumpkin is golden and soft (about 30 minutes) basting frequently.

To make the vinaigrette put the orange juice in a small saucepan and bring to the boil. Reduce for 15 minutes or until you have a syrupy consistency. Mix in the lemon juice, olive oil, salt and pepper.

Toast the pumpkin seeds in a hot, dry frying pan.

Mix the salad leaves with the vinaigrette. On each plate serve a piece of pumpkin with a little sliced mozzarella, dressed watercress leaves, and sprinkle with pumpkin seeds and a little curry powder.

BLACK PUDDING *with* PEARS

Preparation 20 minutes / Cooking 20 minutes

SERVES 4

INGREDIENTS

400 g (14 oz) black pudding
15 g (½ oz) butter

THE PEARS
8 very small pears
50 g (2 oz) butter
50 g (2 oz) sugar
black long pepper (or ordinary peppercorns)

THE GARNISH
100 g (3½ oz) rocket (arugula)
100 g (3½ oz) yellow dandelion leaves (or green)
Lemon Vinaigrette (page 251)

YOU WILL NEED
a mandoline

Wash the pears well but there's no need to peel them. Cut 7 of the pears in half lengthways; set aside the last one.

Melt the butter in a frying pan. Add the sugar and allow it to caramelize slightly. Add the cut pears and cook them in the caramel until well caramelized and soft (5–10 minutes depending on their size and ripeness).

Sprinkle the pears with the ground (or crushed) pepper. Wash the salad leaves.

Fry the black pudding in the butter over a fairly low heat (about 10 minutes, turning it over).

On individual plates arrange the rocket and dandelion leaves, dress with vinaigrette, then top with the cooked pears and the sliced black pudding. With a mandoline, thinly slice the uncooked pear and scatter over the dish.

Poivrade ARTICHOKES

Preparation 20 minutes / Cooking 1 hour

SERVES 4

INGREDIENTS

12 garlic cloves
olive oil
2 sprigs thyme
2 sprigs rosemary
1 bay leaf
8 baby artichokes
juice of 1 lemon
15 g (½ oz) butter

First blanch the garlic: remove the papery white outer layer of the garlic cloves, leaving the last layer of skin on. Immerse the cloves into a pan of boiling water using a slotted spoon and remove after a few seconds. Repeat this process once more – this will sweeten their flavour – then drain.

Put the blanched garlic cloves in a saucepan, cover with oil, add the herbs, leaving aside a few rosemary leaves for later. Simmer gently for 45 minutes. This is your confit.

Break the stalks off from the artichokes, cut off the hard outer leaves and cut off the tops. As you do so, put the prepared artichokes into lemon water to prevent oxidation.

Cut the artichokes in half and remove the chokes, if any. In a frying pan, brown gently in olive oil over a fairly high heat, then add the butter and the rest of the rosemary; cook over a more moderate heat for 7–8 minutes until tender but still firm to the bite.

When it has finished cooking, add the garlic confit and serve.

You can make a little extra garlic confit and keep it in a jar in the fridge, covered with its oil.

STAUB

BEER
CLUB

Interior and Exterior

PUMPKIN *Boulangère*

Preparation 35 minutes / Cooking 1 hour

SERVES 4

INGREDIENTS

- 1 kg (2 lb 3 oz) pumpkin (unpeeled weight)
- 3 tablespoons olive oil
- 1 teaspoon curry powder
- 1 kg (2 lb 3 oz) sweet onions
- 2 garlic cloves
- 2–3 sprigs thyme
- 2 bay leaves
- 150 ml (5 fl oz) chicken stock, or vegetable stock
- 150 g (5 oz) Stilton or other blue cheese
- 2 tablespoons marrow or pumpkin seeds
- sea salt and freshly ground black pepper

Cut the pumpkin into thin slices 5 mm (¼ in) thick and peel. Fry the slices over a fairly high heat in 1 tablespoon of olive oil for about 2 minutes on each side. Add the curry powder and some salt to taste.

Peel and finely slice the sweet onions, then fry very gently over a fairly low heat in the remaining olive oil with the chopped garlic, thyme and bay leaves, for about 25 minutes. Season well with pepper and set aside.

Preheat the oven to 190°C (375°F/Gas 4). In a gratin dish, arrange alternate layers of pumpkin and onion, then pour over the chicken stock. Sprinkle with crumbled Stilton and the marrow seeds. Bake in the oven for about 20 minutes.

STAUB

French-style PEAS

Preparation 30 minutes / Cooking 30 minutes

SERVES 4–6

INGREDIENTS

1.5 kg (3 lb 5 oz) fresh peas, un-podded (approx. 600 g/ 1 lb 5 oz podded)
125 g (4 oz) smoked streaky bacon
1 salad or little gem lettuce
4–5 small spring onions (scallions)
200 ml (7 fl oz) chicken stock (or vegetable stock)
15 g (½ oz) butter

Pod the peas. Boil in a large saucepan of salted water for about 4 minutes; they should remain firm and crunchy.

Drain and cool immediately in iced water.

Cut the smoked streaky bacon into lardons and thinly slice the lettuce and spring onions. Sweat the lardons gently in a large frying pan for 3–4 minutes over a low heat, then add the onions and the lettuce and cook very gently for 4–5 minutes until translucent.

Add the peas to the pan and pour in the chicken stock and butter, mix well. The sauce should be slightly thickened, neither too thick nor too runny. Cover and allow to cook gently for 10 minutes. It should be a syrupy consistency; if it's too thin, continue cooking a little longer.

STAUB
the BEEF CLUB
CHAMPAGNE
CHAMPAGNE
CHAMPAGNE
MORGON
CASCINA FRANCIA
TOUJOURS
STAUB

ASPARAGUS *with* MARROWBONE

Preparation 1 day + 35 minutes / Cooking 24 minutes

SERVES 4

INGREDIENTS

2–3 marrowbones
24 green asparagus spears
2 tablespoons olive oil
fleur de sel
½ bunch flat-leaf parsley
200 g (7 oz) rocket (arugula)
12 Dried Tomatoes (page 253), or shop-bought sun-dried tomatoes

YOU WILL NEED
a mandoline

The day before you want to serve this dish, soak the marrowbones in cold water. Replace the water several times – it should be clear after the 24 hours.

Do not peel the asparagus but remove the spikes with a knife. If they are fat, cut off the woody end of the stalk.

Immerse the asparagus in a large pan of boiling salted water for 4 minutes, then cool immediately in iced water. Cut them into thin slices (about 3 mm/⅛ in) with a mandoline.

Poach the marrowbones in boiling water for 20 minutes, then cool in iced water. Take out the marrow from the bones and cut into slices about 1 cm (½ in) thick.

Arrange the asparagus and slices of marrow in a dish, drizzle with olive oil, and season with fleur de sel. Add the parsley, rocket leaves, and dried tomatoes.

STAUB
STAUB

BLACK TURNIPS

Preparation 20 minutes / Cooking 30 minutes

SERVES 6

INGREDIENTS

1 onion
2 carrots
2 celery stalks
2 garlic cloves
4 Pardailhan or Caluire turnips (alternatively, use round turnips or even black or oriental radishes)
2 tablespoons olive oil
75 ml (2½ fl oz)red wine
2 tablespoons tomato purée (paste)
250 ml (8½ fl oz) chicken stock (or vegetable stock)
2 sprigs of thyme
2 bay leaves
100 g (3½ oz) smoked streaky bacon

Peel the onion, carrots and celery, then cut into approximately 2 mm (⅛ in) dice. Peel and chop the garlic.

Scrub the turnips well and cut into quarters.

In a frying pan, fry the carrots, celery, garlic and onion in the oil over a moderate heat for 4–5 minutes. Add the tomato purée and brown the vegetables, allowing the mixture to reduce until it begins to stick to the bottom of the pan (1–2 minutes).

Deglaze the pan by pouring in the red wine and thoroughly scraping the bottom of the pan. Stir well and add the chicken stock, thyme, bay leaves and turnips.

Cover and cook the turnips over a low heat for about 20 minutes, until nice and soft.

Remove the lid 5 minutes before the end of cooking and increase the heat a little to reduce the liquid.

In the meantime, cut the smoked streaky bacon cut into lardons and fry for 5 minutes, then serve together with the turnips.

STAUB
STAUB

ENDIVE, RADICCHIO & *Watercress with Nuts*

Preparation 30 minutes / Cooking 30 minutes

SERVES 6

INGREDIENTS

1 bunch of watercress
2 red endives
2 yellow endives
½ radicchio
1 egg white
pinch of salt
50 g (2 oz) walnuts
50 g (2 oz) cashew nuts
Grape Vinaigrette (page 251)

Wash all the salad leaves. Pick over the watercress and discard any hard stalks or spoiled leaves. Remove any spoiled or soft outer leaves of the endives and radicchio. Cut into fine strips.

Preheat the oven to 130°C (275°F/Gas 1).

Lightly beat the egg white in a small bowl with a pinch of salt (just enough to make it slightly foamy, not stiff). Add the walnuts and cashew nuts, stir to coat them well. Spread the mixture on a baking tray lined with greaseproof paper and dry in the oven for 30 minutes.

Serve the salad leaves mixed with the nuts, and drizzle with the grape vinaigrette at the last minute.

BRUNCHES

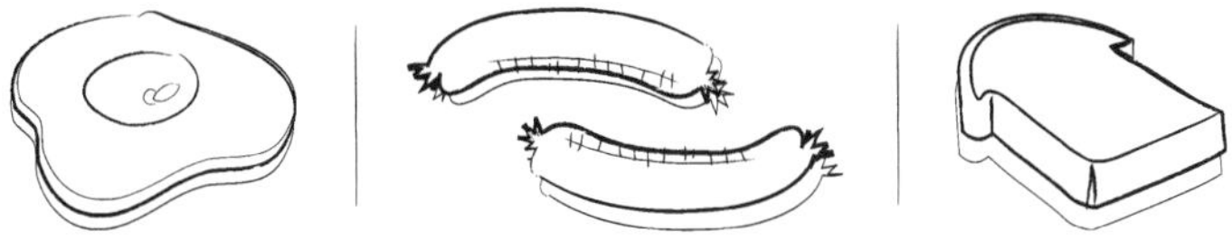

SCONES

Preparation 1 hour 20 minutes / Cooking 15 minutes

MAKES 6 SCONES

INGREDIENTS

120 g (4½ oz) wholemeal flour
125 g (4½ oz) plain (all-purpose) flour, plus a little to sprinkle on the work surface
50 g (2 oz) sugar
1 sachet of baking powder (approx. 10 g/½ oz or 2 teaspoons)
pinch of salt
190 g (6¾ oz) ricotta
80 g double (heavy) cream
120 g (4 g) softened butter

Preheat the oven to 220°C/430°F/Gas 7). Mix all the dry ingredients together in a large bowl or the bowl of a food processor. In a separate bowl, mix the ricotta and cream together.

Incorporate the butter into the dry mixture with your fingertips (or using the food processor). Add the ricotta and cream mixture. Work together quickly with a spatula, without overworking the dough.

Place the ball of dough on a floured surface. Press down with the palm of your hand, but not too hard as you want to maintain a crumbly consistency.

Roll out with a rolling pin or by hand to form a circle 4 cm (1½ in) thick, then cut into 6 equal pieces. Place on baking parchment and leave to rest in the fridge for 1 hour, covered with a tea towel.

If possible, it is best to prepare the dough the day before you bake it. Slide the scones on to a baking tray and bake for 15 minutes.

Delicious served warm with clotted cream and jam or butter and marmalade.

PANCAKES

Preparation 1 hour / Cooking 15 minutes /

MAKES 15 PANCAKES

INGREDIENTS

120 g (4¼ oz) plain (all-purpose) flour
1 teaspoon baking powder
½ teaspoon bicarbonate of soda (baking soda)
30 g (1 oz) caster (superfine) sugar
pinch of salt
240 g (8½ oz) buttermilk
1 large egg
50 g (2 oz) butter
maple syrup

Mix all the dry ingredients together in a large bowl. In a separate bowl, whisk the buttermilk and egg together. Pour this into the dry mixture and stir gently to combine the ingredients without working them too much. Leave to rest at room temperature for 30 minutes.

Heat a large non-stick frying pan over a medium heat, drop in a knob of butter and pour in small ladlefuls of the batter to form pancakes. The batter should immediately start to brown.

As soon as small bubbles begin to form on the surface, flip the pancake over and cook for a further minute or so, to brown the other side. Remove from the pan and pile on a warm plate with a little bit of butter on each pancake; keep warm under aluminium foil. Butter the frying pan again and continue with the rest of the batter. Serve with butter and maple syrup.

ALMOND
TARTLETS
with Blueberries

Preparation 25 minutes / Cooking 15 minutes

MAKES 10 LITTLE ALMOND TARTLETS

INGREDIENTS

8 eggs
100 g (3½ oz) icing (confectioners') sugar
200 g (7 oz) finely ground almonds
200 g (7 oz) soft butter
200 g (7 oz) caster (superfine) sugar
400 g (14 oz) single (half-and-half) cream
50 g (2 oz) butter, for greasing
a little plain (all-purpose) flour, for the work surface
250 g (9 oz) puff pastry
600 g (1 lb 5 oz) fresh blueberries
75 g (2½ oz) dried cranberries
60 g (2¼ oz) flaked (slivered) almonds

YOU WILL NEED
10 cm (4 in) pastry cutter
20 small fluted brioche moulds (small round moulds)

Make an almond cream by whisking together 4 of the eggs with the icing sugar, to whiten the mixture. Add the ground almonds, then the 200 g (7 oz) soft butter, and mix well.

Whisk together the other 4 eggs with the caster sugar, until the mixture becomes white and frothy. Incorporate the single cream and the almond cream. Mix well.

Preheat the oven to 180°C (350°F/Gas 4) and grease the moulds with the butter.

Roll the pastry out on a floured surface, and using a 10 cm (4 in) pastry cutter or a glass, cut into 10 circles. Prick with a fork and line the cake moulds with the pastry. Distribute the blueberries and cranberries evenly between the tartlets. Cover with the almond cream mixture to the edge.

Sprinkle with flaked almonds and bake for 15 minutes.

Remove from the moulds while still hot and serve warm.

BRIOCHE FRENCH *Toast*

Preparation 30 minutes / Cooking 25 minutes

SERVES 4

INGREDIENTS

2 golden delicious apples
40 g (1½ oz) caster (superfine) sugar
45 g (1¾ oz) butter
100 g (3½ oz) muscovado sugar (or light brown sugar)
100 g (3½ oz) water
4 tablespoons thick crème fraîche
4 thick slices of brioche

FRENCH TOAST MIXTURE
300 ml (10 fl oz) milk
160 g (5½ oz) single (half-and-half) cream
½ a vanilla pod (bean)
25 g (1 oz) caster (superfine) sugar
2 eggs

Peel the apples, remove the cores and cut into large pieces.

Put the caster sugar into a frying pan and stir over a medium heat until completely melted. When the sugar begins to caramelize, add 30 g (1 oz) of the butter and let it melt. Add the apples and cook for 5 minutes without stirring, then stir to coat the apples and continue to cook 10 minutes over a fairly low heat.

Whisk together in a bowl all the ingredients for the French toast mixture.

Make a caramel with muscovado sugar and water: put in a saucepan and cook until you have a nice thick syrup.

Soak the slices of brioche in the muscovado caramel for 10 minutes. Heat the remaining butter in a frying pan; when it foams, put in the slices of brioche. Fry the brioche and when one side is nice and golden, turn it over to brown the other. Do this in several batches if the frying pan is not big enough to do them all at once.

Arrange a slice of brioche on each plate. Add a spoonful of crème fraîche, some chunks of apple, and pour over the muscovado sugar caramel (reheat if it has gone too hard).

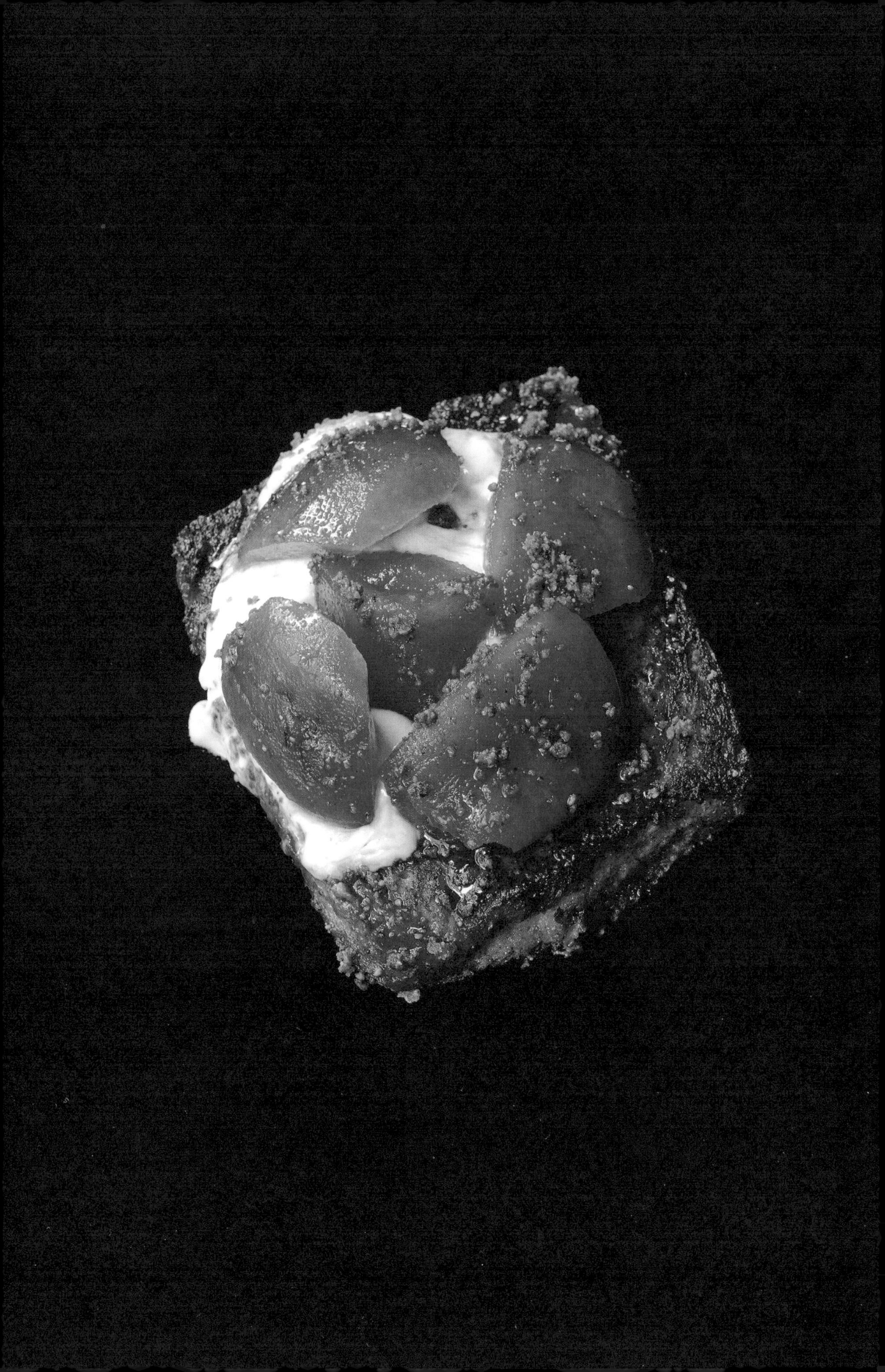

GRANOLA

Preparation 15 minutes / Cooking 45 minutes

SERVES 4

INGREDIENTS

- 15 g (½ oz) pecans
- 15 g (½ oz) cashew nuts
- 15 g (½ oz) hazelnuts
- 100 g (3½ oz) mixed cereal flakes
- 40 g (1½ oz) maple syrup plus a little for decoration
- 40 g (1½ oz) corn syrup or agave syrup (or runny honey)
- 1 pineapple
- 1 mango
- 2 kiwi fruits
- 2 bananas
- 4 creamy yoghurts
- 2 passion fruits
- 40 g (1½ oz) dried cranberries
- 15 g (½ oz) coconut flakes
- a few small shortbread biscuits to serve (optional)

Preheat the oven to 140°C (275°F/Gas 1). Crush all of the nuts and mix with the cereal flakes.

Heat the maple syrup with the corn syrup gently in a small saucepan. Pour over the cereal and nut mixture, and stir until coated. Spread this mixture on a baking tray covered with greaseproof paper and bake in the oven for 45 minutes. Allow to cool (it will keep for several days in an airtight container).

To serve, peel the pineapple, mango, kiwi fruits and bananas, then cut into cubes. Put yoghurt in the bottom of 4 bowls, arrange the fruit cubes, sprinkle with granola, add the pulp of the passion fruits (cut them in half and scoop out the pulp with a spoon). Add a little maple syrup, the cranberries, coconut flakes, and the shortbread biscuits.

the BEEF CLUB
SIDES
BRUNCH MENU
BOUTEILLE CHAMPAGNE
BILLECART SALMON
- 45€ -
SCONES
FOUR PANCAKES
TOASTS

THE BEST OF
Profiterole

EGGS
Benedict

Preparation 20 minutes / Cooking 15 minutes

SERVES 4

INGREDIENTS

- 4 white English muffins
- 8 slices of bacon (or smoked streaky bacon)
- 10 g (½ oz) butter
- 150 ml (5 fl oz) spirit vinegar
- 8 very fresh eggs (freshness is important)
- Hollandaise Sauce (page 252)
- 20 g (¾ oz) crushed toasted hazelnuts
- Espelette pepper

Lightly toast the halved muffins under the grill or in a toaster.

Fry the bacon in a frying pan with the butter, until nice and crispy (about 5 minutes).

Bring 1 litre (34 fl oz) of water with the spirit vinegar to a gentle boil in a saucepan. Break an egg into a ramekin. Slide the egg into the water to poach it; repeat the process with the remaining eggs (do this in batches if the saucepan is small). Lower the heat and cook for 3 minutes. Take the eggs out with a slotted spoon and set them on the bottom half of each muffin. Garnish with sauce, bacon, some pepper and toasted hazelnuts, then replace the muffin tops.

TOSTADA *de* GAMBAS

Preparation 1 day + 2 hours 25 minutes / Cooking 5 minutes

SERVES 4

INGREDIENTS

8 large tiger prawns (shrimps)
juice and zest of 1 lime
100 ml (3 ½ fl oz) olive oil
salt
4 corn tortillas
Spicy Mayonnaise Sauce (page 251)

THE GUACAMOLE
2 ripe avocados
1 lime
1 garlic clove, chopped
1 sweet red (bell) pepper, diced
pinch of cumin
pinch of Espelette pepper

THE SALAD
handful of salad leaves of your choice
½ red onion
½ bunch of coriander (cilantro)
1 sweet green (bell) pepper

Remove the heads of the prawns, shell them, and cut into pieces 5 mm (¼ in) thick. Put them to marinate in the juice and grated zest of 1 lime, olive oil and a pinch salt, for at least 2 hours or, better still, 24 hours.

For the guacamole, scoop out the flesh from the avocados and crush roughly in a bowl with a fork. Add the lime juice, chopped garlic and red pepper, as well as the cumin and Espelette pepper.

Mix the salad leaves with the finely sliced onion, chopped coriander and finely sliced green pepper.

Griddle the corn tortillas in a hot griddle pan, then spread a little guacamole on top. Add the prawn pieces, a little mayonnaise, and top with the salad.

the BEEF CLUB
BRUNCH MENU
DESSERTS
SUNDAY's SUNDAYS

Cobb SALAD

Preparation 30 minutes / Cooking 20 minutes

SERVES 4

INGREDIENTS

- 2 free-range chicken thighs, preferably deboned
- sea salt and freshly ground black pepper
- 1 teaspoon grapeseed oil
- 1 romaine lettuce
- 4 eggs
- 1 red onion
- 2 ripe avocados
- juice of ½ lemon
- 100 g (3½ oz) stilton (or other blue-veined cheese)
- 8 thin slices of dry-cured smoked bacon
- 4 Dried Tomatoes (page 253), or shop-bought

THE VINAIGRETTE

- 4 tablespoons olive oil
- 125 ml (4 fl oz) grapeseed oil
- 4 tablespoons red wine vinegar
- 2 tablespoons water
- ½ lemon
- ½ teaspoon Worcestershire sauce
- 1 teaspoon Dijon mustard
- good pinch of sugar
- good pinch of salt
- good pinch of white pepper
- 1 crushed garlic clove
- ½ tablespoon maple syrup
- ½ tablespoon fish sauce (such as nam pla)

Beat together all the vinaigrette ingredients in a bowl or put them in a tightly closed jar and shake vigorously. There will inevitably be some vinaigrette left over for another recipe.

Preheat the oven grill to 200°C (400°F/Gas 6). Debone the chicken if required. Season, coat with the oil and grill for 10 minutes, turning once. Slice the chicken into thin slivers.

While the chicken is cooking, wash the lettuce. Pile up the leaves and slice into broad strips.

Boil the eggs for 6 minutes until soft-boiled, cool in ice-cold water, then gently remove the shells.

Peel and thinly slice the onion. Peel and cut the avocados into dice and sprinkle lightly with lemon juice. Cut the stilton into chunks.

Brown the slices of bacon in a frying pan until golden and crisp; drain on kitchen paper.

On each plate, arrange the chicken, stilton, avocado, dried tomatoes, onion, the bacon torn into strips, and the eggs cut into quarters. Serve the vinaigrette on the side.

GALLOWAY
LONGHORN
SHORTHORN
the
BEEF
CLUB
POISSONS
HOMARD
LANGOUSTINE
SCOTCH EGG DORÉ AU
& jeunes pousses en salade
JOUE DE BOEUF & FOI
en terrine, vinaigrette aux lenti
PALOURDES & CHA
cuites au four, ail &
LANGOUSTINES B
croustillantes, rémoulade
& moutarde
CAVIAR /
- Les plat
Pièces de boeuf de la fe
à l'herbe. Les p
ENTRECÔTE (en
CÔTE DE BOEU
FILET DE BOEU
UX-FILET (en
ISTECK (env 25
the BE
Boeuf hach
bacon, oignons
& sauce maison au wh

PIG TROTTER *Tartines*

Preparation 1 hour 25 minutes / Cooking 3 h 30

SERVES 4

INGREDIENTS

- 2 pig trotters
- 1 tablespoon pork rillettes (or potted pork)
- 1 tablespoon wholegrain mustard
- 3 sprigs tarragon, chopped
- 1 shallot, chopped
- 4 slices of sourdough bread
- 1 garlic clove, halved
- 125 g (4 oz) Montgomery's Cheddar (or other good Cheddar or Cantal cheese)

THE STOCK

- 1 carrot
- 1 onion
- 1 leek
- 1 stick celery
- 1 teaspoon dried coriander
- 2 cloves
- 1 teaspoon white pepper
- 2 garlic cloves
- 2 sprigs thyme
- 2 bay leaves
- sea salt and freshly ground black pepper

Blanch the pig trotters in a pot of salted water for 10 minutes. Leave to cool. Wipe to remove any impurities.

Make the stock by washing and, where necessary, peeling carrot, onion, leek and celery. Put the vegetables into a large saucepan or stockpot and add the rest of the stock ingredients along with the trotters. Cover the contents with water, bring to the boil on a high heat and then reduce the heat. Simmer gently for 3 hours until soft.

Allow to cool in the stock for about 1 hour. Drain.

Preheat the oven to 160°C (320°F/Gas 3).

Remove the skin from the trotters to access the meat and gelatinous parts; remove any cartilage. Chop the meat finely. Mix with the rillettes, mustard, chopped tarragon and shallot in a bowl and season.

Toast the bread on one side only, then rub the toasted side with the cut-side of the garlic clove. Spread with the trotter and rillette mixture, sprinkle with the grated cheese and put in the oven for 10 minutes.

ORANGE
SALAD

Preparation 1 day + 25 minutes / Cooking 5 minutes

SERVES 4

INGREDIENTS

THE PICKLED CARROTS
2 bunches of young carrots
100 ml (3½ fl oz) water
1 tablespoon sugar
100 ml (3½ fl oz) spirit vinegar

THE ORANGES
6 blood oranges
1 red onion
40 g (1½ oz) taggiasche olives
(or other good black olives)
50 g (2 oz) rocket (arugula)
a few sprigs of parsley
2 tablespoons olive oil
salt

YOU WILL NEED
a mandoline

Clean the carrots and cut into thin rounds with the mandoline (or with a knife). Bring to a simmer in a saucepan of the water, sugar and vinegar. Add the carrots and, as soon as it returns to a simmer, turn off the heat and allow to cool. Pour the carrots and liquid into a jar and leave to pickle for 24 hours if possible.

Peel and remove the pith and inner membrane of the oranges and keep a little skin aside for the zest. Cut the segments without taking any pith.

Arrange on each plate some orange segments, finely sliced red onion, pitted and sliced olives, rocket leaves, parsley and a few pickled carrot rounds. Drizzle with olive oil, salt, and finely grate over a little orange zest.

the
BEEF
CLUB
BRUNCH MENU
SUNDAY'S
SUNDAYS
(la coupe)
(la coupe)
45€ (bouteille)
60€ (bouteille)
70€ (bouteille)
90€ (bouteille)
90€ (bouteille)

MULTICOLOURED BEETROOT *Salad*

Preparation 20 minutes / Cooking 45 minutes

SERVES 6

INGREDIENTS

500 g (1 lb 2 oz) yellow beetroots (beets)
500 g (1 lb 2 oz) white beetroots (beets)
500 g (1 lb 2 oz) Chioggia beetroots (beets)
30 g (1 oz) marrow or pumpkin seeds
2 teaspoons olive oil
sea salt and freshly ground black pepper
Lemon Vinaigrette (page 251)
200 g (7 oz) firm goats' cheese

Clean the beetroots well by scrubbing them under running water, but do not peel. Cook all the beetroots together, in their skins, in a large saucepan of salted water for about 40 minutes (the time will depend on their size). Prick them with the tip of a knife to check when cooked; they should yield easily to the knife.

Leave to cool just long enough to be able to handle them. Peel them (the skin will come away easily) and cut into cubes.

Toast the marrow seeds for a few minutes in a hot frying pan with a little oil, salt and pepper. As soon as they split and begin to brown, pour into a bowl. Take care, it is easy to burn them.

Gently mix together the beetroots and the vinaigrette. Sprinkle with cubes of cheese and marrow seeds, then serve.

DESSERTS

Chocolate SUNDAE

Preparation 15 minutes / Cooking 15 minutes

SERVES 4

INGREDIENTS

- 4 tablespoons peanut butter
- 15–20 mini salted pretzels
- 1 banana
- Chantilly Cream (page 253)
- 4 large scoops of chocolate ice cream
- Caramel Sauce (page 253)

Gently heat the peanut butter in a small saucepan to make it slightly runny.

Break up the pretzels. Cut the banana into small chunks.

Layer in each glass or tall dish some Chantilly cream, a scoop of ice cream, some peanut butter sauce, some caramel sauce, and some more Chantilly cream, chunks of banana and broken pieces of pretzel.

Vanilla SUNDAE

Preparation 30 minutes / Cooking 35 minutes

SERVES 4

INGREDIENTS

4 scoops of vanilla ice cream

THE BROWNIE
120 g (4 oz) butter, plus a little for the cake tin
200 g (7 oz) muscovado sugar (or soft brown sugar)
120 g (4 oz) maple syrup
250 g (9 oz) dark chocolate
4 eggs
95 g (3¼ oz) plain (all-purpose) flour
30 g (1 oz) cocoa powder
½ teaspoon salt
95 g (3¼ oz) pecan nuts, roughly chopped

THE CHOCOLATE SAUCE
100 ml (3½ fl oz) water
50 g (2 oz) sugar
110 g (3¾ oz) dark chocolate
1 tablespoon whisky
Chantilly Cream (page 253)
Caramel Sauce (page 253)

To make the brownie, preheat the oven to 160°C (320°F/Gas 3).

Heat together the butter, sugar and maple syrup in a saucepan to near boiling point.

Pour this almost boiling mixture on to the chocolate broken into small chunks in a bowl and whisk until smooth. Incorporate the eggs and stir carefully. Sift together the flour, salt and cocoa powder, and fold in. Add the chopped pecans.

Pour the mixture into a buttered baking tin lined with greaseproof paper. Bake for 20 minutes.

Leave to cool then cut into small pieces.

For the chocolate sauce, mix the water and sugar in a small saucepan, bring to the boil stirring to dissolve the sugar. Remove from the heat and add the whisky, then the chocolate in pieces, and stir well until smooth.

Into each glass or tall dish layer some caramel sauce, a scoop of ice cream, some chocolate sauce and some Chantilly cream.

Top with the pieces of brownie and a drizzle of caramel and chocolate sauce.

Profiteroles

Preparation 1 hour / Cooking 1 hour

SERVES 6

INGREDIENTS

THE CRAQUELIN
30 g (1 oz) butter
35 g (1¼ oz) light brown sugar
35 g (1¼ oz) plain (all-purpose) flour

THE CHOUX PASTRY
200 ml (7 fl oz) water
110 g (3¾ oz) butter
pinch of salt
1 teaspoon sugar
100 g (3½ oz) plain (all-purpose) flour
pinch of baking powder
3 eggs

THE CHOCOLATE SAUCE
100 ml (3¾ fl oz) water
50 g (2 oz) sugar
zest of ½ lemon
zest of ½ lime
zest of 1 small orange
1 tablespoon whisky
110 g (3¾ oz) dark chocolate

THE PRALINE FEUILLETINE
60 g (2 oz) dark chocolate
200 g (7 oz) praline (caramelized ground hazelnuts and sugar)
60 g (2 oz) crushed crêpes dentelles (crispy fine crêpes)

THE CARAMELIZED PECANS
50 g (2 oz) pecans
100 g (3½ oz) sugar

500 ml (17 fl oz) vanilla ice cream, to serve
homemade Chantilly cream (page 253), to serve

YOU WILL NEED
pastry cutter
piping bag

Mix together all the craquelin ingredients to form a nice smooth pastry. Roll it out between 2 sheets of baking parchment, until very thin (2–3 mm (⅛ in) maximum).

Leave to rest on a tray in the freezer for 30 minutes, then cut into circles with a pastry cutter.

The discs should match the size of the choux buns you are making. Preheat the oven to 165°C (330°F).

Now make the choux pastry. Put the water, butter cut into chunks, salt and sugar into a saucepan. Bring to the boil. Remove from the heat, pour in the flour and baking powder together, and stir vigorously. Return to a low heat and stir constantly until the pastry is dry and comes away from the side of the pan. Transfer to a large bowl and leave to cool for 5 minutes.

Incorporate the eggs one by one with a spatula. The pastry should be malleable but not runny: you may not need all 3 eggs, just enough to achieve the desired consistency. Shape 6 large individual choux buns with the piping bag on a tray covered with greaseproof paper. Put a disc of craquelin on each bun and bake for 30 minutes. Allow to cool with the oven door half open.

For the chocolate sauce, in a small saucepan bring the water and sugar to a boil stirring to dissolve the sugar. Add the citrus zests and simmer for 5 minutes. Add the whisky. Remove from the heat and add the pieces of chocolate and stir well until smooth.

For the prailine feuilletine, melt the chocolate with the praline in a bain-marie. Add the crêpes dentelles and stir.

To caramalize the pecans, roast the pecans spread out on a baking tray for 6–7 minutes in an oven preheated to 190°C (375°F/Gas 5). Chop them roughly. Put the sugar in a small saucepan with a little water, heat until you have a pale caramel, remove from the heat and add the chopped nuts. Pour on to a baking tray covered with baking parchment and leave to set, then break into pieces.

Reheat the chocolate sauce in a bain-marie. Cut each choux bun in half horizontally. Spread a little praline feuilletine on the base, add a scoop of ice cream, a little Chantilly cream (you will not use all of it) and close the choux bun. Drizzle a little chocolate sauce and pieces of caramelized broken pecan nuts over the top.

APPLE
Tartlets

Preparation 30 minutes / Cooking 2 hours 30 minutes

MAKES 4 TARTLETS

INGREDIENTS

8 golden delicious apples
150 g (5 oz) caster (superfine) sugar
120 ml (4 fl oz) of water
juice of ½ lemon
1 roll of puff pastry (250 g/9 oz)
150 g (5 oz) butter

Peel 4 of the apples, remove the cores and cut into slices. Put in a saucepan with 50 g (2 oz) of the sugar, the water and lemon juice. Allow to stew on a very low heat for 2 hours then stir.

Roll out the pastry and cut into 15 cm (6 in) diameter discs. Prick with a fork and put 1 tablespoon of apple compote on each one.

Peel the other 4 apples, remove the cores and cut into thin slices about 2 mm (⅛ in) thick. Arrange them attractively in a circular pattern on the tartlet bases.

Clarify the butter by melting it gently; when it boils, skim off the foam on the surface. Brush the tarts with clarified butter and sprinkle with some of the remaining sugar.

Put the tarts in the oven at 180°C (350°F/Gas 4) for about 30 minutes. Midway through the baking, take them out and brush again with butter and the rest of the sugar.

RUM BABAS

Preparation 2 hours 35 minutes / Cooking 1 hour 45 minutes

MAKES 4 INDIVIDUAL BABAS

INGREDIENTS

THE BABA PASTRY
150 g (5 oz) plain (all-purpose) flour
125 g (4 oz) caster (superfine) sugar
3 g (½ teaspoon) salt
1 sachet of dried yeast (7 g/¼ oz)
65 g (2¼ oz) milk, warmed
2 eggs
50 g (2 oz) butter at room temperature plus a little for the moulds

THE SYRUP
500 ml (17 fl oz) water
75 g (2½ oz) caster (superfine) sugar
1 star anise
1 small cinnamon stick
2 cardamom seeds
1 clove
1 vanilla pod (bean)
1 lemongrass stalk
110 ml (3¾ fl oz) amber rum

THE STEWED LEMONS
2 unwaxed lemons
100 g (3 ½ oz) sugar
200 g (7 oz) water

Chantilly Cream (page 253), to serve
lemon balm leaves, to garnish
rum, to drizzle

YOU WILL NEED
4 individual baba moulds or one big one

For the pastry, mix the dry ingredients in a large bowl or the bowl of a food processor. Add the warm milk and the eggs. Incorporate using the food mixer hook or a flat whisk – or a spoon and elbow grease! Knead until you have a nice smooth dough (if you don't have a food processor, you can knead the dough in the bowl).

Add the butter and knead some more. Divide the dough into the well-buttered baba tins. Cover with cling film (plastic wrap) and leave the dough to rise (preferably in a warm place, 25–30°C (75–85°F), such as near a radiator, and away from draughts) for 1 hour. The dough should double in volume.

Preheat the oven to 170°C (340°F/Gas 3½). Bake the babas in the oven for 35 minutes; they should be nice and dry.

Make the syrup by mixing the water and sugar in a small saucepan. Bring to the boil, stirring to dissolve the sugar. Remove from the heat, add the spices, vanilla, lemongrass and rum, cover and allow to infuse for 15 minutes.

Take the babas out of the moulds, soak in the strained syrup in a bowl, leaving them for 20 minutes without turning them over.

For the stewed lemons, peel the lemon zest without any pith with a peeler and slice into strips. Blanch them by immersing in boiling water for 1 minute, drain then rinse in cold water.

Mix the water and sugar in a saucepan, bring to the boil, stirring, then add the zests and stew them gently for 1 hour. Drain them and add a squeeze of lemon juice.

Serve the babas topped with Chantilly cream, garnished with the lemon zest and lemon balm cut into fine strips. Pour over a drizzle of rum.

STRAWBERRY

Tarts

Preparation 42 hours 10 minutes / Cooking 1 hour 12 minutes

SERVES 4

INGREDIENTS

THE SWEET PASTRY
85 g (3 oz) salted butter
90 g (3¼ oz) caster (superfine) sugar
1 egg yolk
½ vanilla pod (bean)
100 g (3½ oz) plain (all-purpose) flour plus a little for the worktop
1½ teaspoons baking powder

THE BAVAROIS AND THE COULIS
500 g (1 lb 2 oz) strawberries
100 g (3½ oz) water
9 sheets of gelatine
150 g (5 oz) single (half-and-half) cream

400 g (14 oz) strawberries (preferably small ones)
2 tablespoons pistachios unroasted and unsalted, finely ground

For the pastry, beat together the butter and sugar. Add the egg yolk and the seeds from the vanilla pod (split the vanilla pod and scrape the seeds out with a knife). Then fold in the flour mixed with the baking powder. Knead into pastry and leave to rest in a cold place for at least 1 hour.

Preheat the oven to 170°C (340°F/Gas 3½).

Roll the pastry out very thin on a lightly floured worktop. Cut out circles 10 cm (4 in) in diameter. Place them on a baking tray covered with greaseproof paper. Bake for 12 minutes, then leave to cool.

Now make the bavarois and coulis. Stew 250 g (19 oz) of the strawberries (de-stalked) with water in a saucepan over a gentle heat for 1 hour. Blend. Add the remaining 250 g of strawberries (stalks removed) and blend again. Put the gelatin in cold water to soften, then drain and incorporate into the strawberry mixture with a whisk. Weigh the mixture, take half of it and set aside; add the other half to the cream in a separate bowl. Leave the 2 mixtures to cool (but not set) for about 30 minutes.

Arrange a layer of the bavarois mixture (with the cream) on the tart bases using a piping bag or a spoon. Place the fresh strawberrie (de-stalked, and cut in half if large) on top, then add the coulis mixture (without cream) and sprinkle with the ground pistachio.

the BEEF CLUB
POISSONS
HOMARD
LANGOUSTINE
Boeuf haché sur
bacon, oignons grillés
& sauce maison au whisky

Red BERRIES AND CREAM

Preparation 1 hour 25 minutes / Cooking 20 minutes

SERVES 6

INGREDIENTS

60 g (2 oz) caster (superfine) sugar
60 g (2 oz) light brown sugar
60 g (2 oz) butter
65 g (2¼ oz) plain (all-purpose) flour
60 g (2 oz) orange juice
750 ml (25 fl oz) olive oil
½ vanilla pod (bean)
500 g (1 lb 2 oz) strawberries
250 g (9 oz) raspberries
150 g (5 oz) blueberries
100 g red currants
6 scoops of marscapone ice cream
a little icing (confectioners') sugar

Mix together the caster sugar and light brown sugar in a bowl. Melt the butter and add to the sugars, then sift the flour on top, add the orange juice and mix well. Leave this mixture to rest in the fridge for 1 hour.

Preheat the oven to 180°C (350°F/Gas 4). Put small spoonfuls of the mixture on a baking tray covered with greaseproof paper.

Bake in the oven for 12–15 minutes; the tuiles should be nice and golden. Leave to cool for a few minutes and release them from the paper.

Gently heat the olive oil (without boiling) in a small saucepan. Add the scraped seeds from the vanilla pod. Remove from the heat, cover and leave to infuse and cool.

Wash, sort and de-stalk the fruit. Arrange the fruit in dishes with a scoop of ice cream and top with a tuile. Drizzle with vanilla oil. Sprinkle with a little icing sugar.

COCKTAILS

TIPS
FROM THE BARTENDER

IN THE TRADITION OF THE AMERICAN-STYLE STEAKHOUSE, THE BEEF CLUB OFFERS A FINE COCKTAIL LIST, PREPARED IN AUTHENTIC COCKTAIL-MAKING TRADITION BY THE BALLROOM BARTENDER.

THE BALLROOM

The Ballroom is a venue designed for partying.It's The Beef Club's underground bar. In the purest style of the American steakhouse and speakeasies, as the clandestine bars of the prohibition era were known, we wanted to keep the idea of offering an extensive wine list, but also a fine range of cocktails to be enjoyed in a laid-back atmosphere away from prying eyes. This is the Ballroom – well worth a visit before or after the Beef Club. As with our meat, we have selected only the best drinks for the bar.

OUR COCKTAILS

We have a vast collection of spirits, from which we have eliminated industrial products as far as possible. We make ample use of spice mixes and homemade cordials (we make our own grenadine on the premises, for instance).

We use methods and recipes that date from the late 19th century – not without giving them a more contemporary twist, notably with freshly squeezed juices of seasonal fruits, or with fresh herbs. As well as these classic recipes, we have new creations, incorporating rare spices or exotic fruits.

THE BARTENDER'S ROLE

The work of the bartender, these days sometimes known as a mixologist, is as complex and demanding as that of the chef: quantities must be precise and used with delicacy, and techniques must be mastered, while the customer is served in a friendly and relaxed manner. When you are preparing cocktails at home, remember that the way you serve them is as important as the recipe: use the right glass and big fresh ice cubes.

COCKTAILS FOR SHARING

At the Ballroom, we particularly like offering cocktails for sharing, in the tradition of English punch: traditional recipes are served in generous quantities, very much in the spirit of The Beef Club's food.

SPEYMALT
MACALLAN
DISTILLERY
BOURBON CASK
AGED
THE
HAKUSHU
SINGLE MALT
WHISKY
12
白州
SINGLE MALT
余市

METHODS

Cocktails are made in a shaker, a mixing glass or directly in the glass, especially when only a few ingredients are involved.

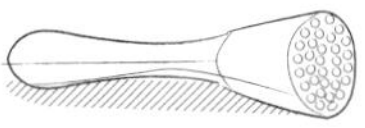
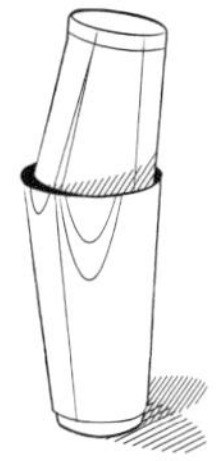

MIXING GLASS

The mixing glass is a large sturdy glass.

The ingredients are added to the glass, then ice cubes are stirred in with a spoon in a circular motion.

It's a traditional technique that allows slower cooling, and is therefore usually used to bring out and preserve the flavour of the spirits as much as possible.

SHAKER

The traditional shaker is made of stainless steel, usually with a built-in strainer. The more traditional Boston Shaker is a two-piece shaker made of metal and glass.

The principle of making cocktails in a shaker is simple: you put the ingredients in the shaker, if necessary crushing the fruits or fresh herbs with a pestle and adding the ice only at the end. Shake it vigorously for a few moments and serve immediately.

Take care not to shake for too long; if the ice melts completely it will leave the mixture with too watery a taste.

THE INGREDIENTS

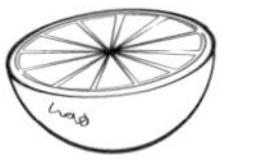

Many of the ingredients used in the Ballroom's cocktails are from traditional recipes.

THE SUGAR SYRUP

You can buy this but it is always better to make your own, and it's very easy! Stir together 500 ml (17 fl oz) hot water and 500 g (1 lb 2 oz) cane sugar until the sugar has completely dissolved.

LEMONS AND LIMES

Lemons and limes must be squeezed at the last minute so they don't oxidize. Take care not to squeeze too hard because the pith of the citrus fruit can make the juice bitter. In general, lemons are more acidic than limes. Sugar is often added to balance the citrus, using 20 ml (1 oz) of citrus juice to 20 ml (1 oz) of sugar syrup.

FRUIT

It is best to choose fruit that is fresh and seasonal; peel it and crush it in the bottom of the shaker. Don't forget to taste as you go to ensure a well-balanced cocktail.

HERBS

Herbs such as mint require particular care because they are fragile. The best method is to cut them or chill them without crushing them, otherwise they lose their flavour.

BITTERS

Bitters are reductions of spices, peels and plants that bring out their flavours. A few drops are enough. The most common one is Angostura, readily available in the shops.

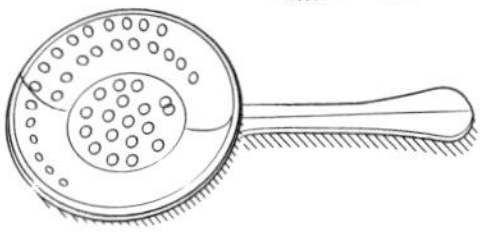

BARTENDER'S TIPS

- For a cocktail made in the glass, keep the mixing glass in your hand; when the temperature feels right, serve.
- The recipes are given in millilitre, gram and ounce measurements. This allows great precision. Preferably use 40 ml (1½ oz)/20 ml (1 oz) or 50 ml (2 oz)/30 ml (1¼ oz). Don't forget that a bar mixing spoon holds 5 ml (1 tsp), for making all the recipes!
- If the shaker doesn't have a built-in strainer, consider using a sieve for the ice, fruit pieces etc., when pouring.

SMOKY

Cucumber

MAKES 1 GLASS

INGREDIENTS

50 ml (2 oz) tequila
25 ml (1 oz) agave syrup
20 ml (1 oz) lime juice
5 ml (1 tsp) cucumber juice (cucumber passed through the juicer with the skin)
5 ml (1 tsp) green chartreuse
3 dashes of mezcal infused with coriander (cilantro) and dried red chilli peppers (place the ingredients in the bottle and leave to infuse; the longer you leave it the stronger the flavour)
20 ml (1 oz) egg white
crushed ice

DECORATION
1 slice of cucumber

YOU WILL NEED
a shaker

Pour all the ingredients except the ice into the shaker and shake once vigorously to create the egg white emulsion, a technique known as dry shaking.

Then fill with as much ice as you can and shake again until frost appears on the surface of the metal tumbler. Pour into a chilled cocktail glass and decorate with a slice of cucumber.

Something of a cross between a Tommy's Margarita and a Tequila Sour, this is a very fresh, slightly acidic and spicy cocktail suitable for any occasion.

Ballroom

MAI TAI

MAKES 1 GLASS

INGREDIENTS

40 ml (1½ oz) rum
20 ml (1 oz) orgeat syrup (homemade or bought)
20 ml (1 oz) lime juice
20 ml (1 oz) dry curaçao
2 dashes of Angostura bitters
5 ml (1 tsp) whisky
ice cubes
crushed ice

DECORATION
1 sprig young mint leaves
zest of 1 orange
1 cherry

YOU WILL NEED
a shaker

Pour all the ingredients into the shaker and shake till frost appears, then filter into a double old-fashioned glass tumbler filled with ice cubes and crushed ice.

Decorate with the tip of a spring of young mint leaves, orange zest and a cherry.

A great classic in the Tiki family, this very fragrant, fruity and sweet cocktail will delight any lover of rums.

PIRATE'S BLOOD

MAKES 1 GLASS

INGREDIENTS

15 ml (3 tsp) Angostura bitters
15 ml (3 tsp) orgeat syrup (homemade or bought)
15 ml (3 tsp) lime juice
15 ml (3 tsp) grapefruit juice
15 ml (3 tsp) fino sherry
30 ml (1¼ oz) whisky
ice cubes

DECORATION
½ lime
1 sugar cube
overproof rum (very strong rum)

YOU WILL NEED
a shaker

Pour all the ingredients into the shaker and shake vigorously until frost appears on the metal tumbler, then filter into a long drink glass filled with crushed glass.

Decorate with half a lime in which you have placed a sugar cube generously soaked in overproof rum (75%) which can be flambéed to dramatic effect in the dark.

Bitter and fruity, this is a great cocktail for winter evenings, when the sun makes itself scarce.

Atomic MARGARITA PUNCH

MAKES 4–5 GLASSES

INGREDIENTS

120 ml (4 oz) tequila
120 ml (4 oz) lime juice
90 ml (3 oz) mezcal
90 ml (3 oz) agave syrup
90 ml (3 oz) Green Chartreuse
6 dashes of mezcal infused with coriander (cilantro) and dried red chilli peppers (place the ingredients in the bottle and leave to infuse; the longer you leave it the stronger the flavour)
ice cubes

DECORATION
4–5 slices of cucumber

YOU WILL NEED
2 shakers

Mix all the ingredients in two shakers, and shake until frost forms on the surface of the metal tumbler, then filter into a chilled decanter to keep the cocktail at as cold a temperature as possible.

Everyone can then serve themselves into an ice-filled glass and top with a slice of cucumber.

Slightly acidic, herby and spicy, this is a cocktail to please lovers of exciting flavour sensations.

Zombie PUNCH

MAKES 4–5 GLASSES

INGREDIENTS

10 ml (2 tsp) grenadine
10 ml (2 tsp) lime liqueur
10 ml (2 tsp) Maraschino
50 ml (2 oz) Myers's rum
50 ml (2 oz) Appleton Estate V/X
50 ml (2 oz) Pusser's
20 ml (1 oz) lime juice
15 ml (3 tsp) grapefruit juice
2 dashes of Angostura bitters
2 dashes of absinthe
ice cubes

DECORATION
1 lime
1 sugar cube

YOU WILL NEED
a shaker

Pour all the ingredients into a shaker and shake well until it reaches the desired, icy, temperature.

Pour into a punch bowl filled with ice and decorate with a torch made from a lime holding a piece of sugar soaked in rum to be lit when serving.

The Zombie is one of the great classics of Donn 'The Beachcomber' Beach, father of the tiki movement in the 1950s.

Fruity and strong, this sharing cocktail will guarantee lovers of exoticism an evening of high spirits.

THE BALLROOM

Drinking, Cosy Atmosphere

Salers SMASH

MAKES 1 GLASS

INGREDIENTS

20 ml (1 oz) sugar syrup
20 ml (1 oz) lemon juice
40 ml (1½ oz) Salers gentian liqueur
Champagne
ice cubes

DECORATION
1 tip of a sprig of mint leaves

YOU WILL NEED
a shaker

Pour the ingredients, except the Champagne, into the shaker and shake until frost appears, then pour into a double old-fashioned glass filled with crushed ice.

Add the Champagne and decorate with the tip of a sprig of fresh mint leaves.

This fresh and sparkling cocktail perfectly sets off the gentle bitterness of the gentian and makes a perfect aperitif.

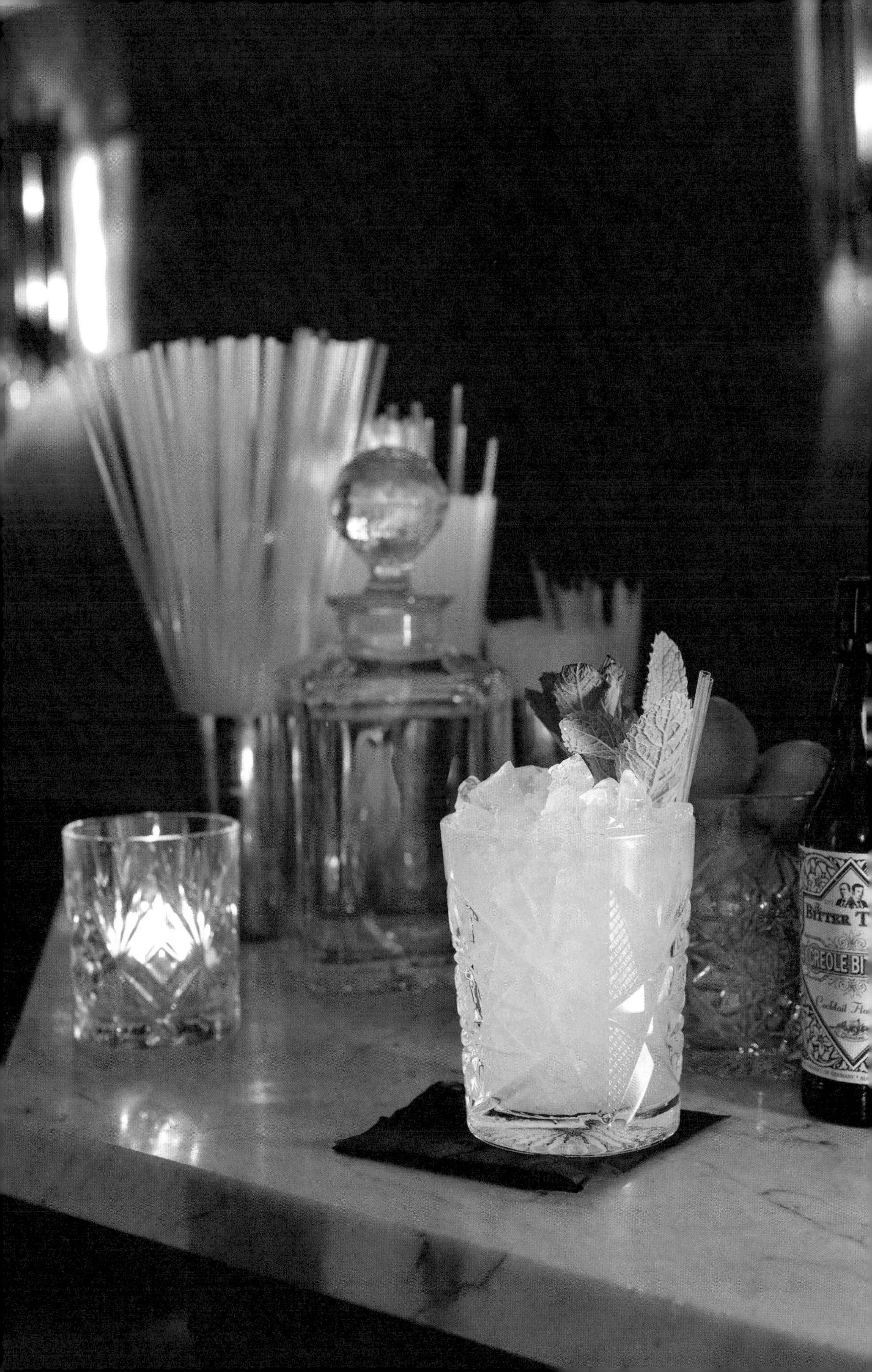

Madame RÊVE

MAKES 1 GLASS

INGREDIENTS

20 ml (1 oz) lemon juice
1 strawberry
50 ml (2 oz) Aperol infused with aniseed, vanilla, clove, cinnamon and nutmeg (put the ingredients in the bottle and leave to infuse; the longer you leave it the stronger the flavour)
Champagne
crushed ice

YOU WILL NEED
a shaker

Crush a nice fresh strawberry in the shaker, then add the lemon juice and the infused Aperol; shake vigorously until frost appears, then filter twice into a chilled cocktail glass.

Add the champagne, and serve with a smile.

This fresh and fruity cocktail will delight the women and surprise the men.

Nepali JULEP

MAKES 1 GLASS

INGREDIENTS

5 ml (1 tsp) syrup of cinnamon and Timur pepper from Nepal (you can also use Sichuan pepper)
50 ml (2 fl oz) gin
10 ml (2 teaspoons) Picon
crushed ice
1 sprig fresh mint leaves
1 pipette Cherry Heering liqueur
ice cubes, roughly broken

Make the syrup by heating 200 ml (7 oz) water and 200 g (7 oz) sugar, stirring to dissolve the sugar. Add a small stick of cinnamon and a few crushed Timur peppercorns.

Cover and leave to infuse until it has cooled. Filter (you will of course have more than enough for one person).

Pour the cinnamon syrup along with the gin and Picon into a julep cup style of tumbler, half fill with crushed ice and stir generously.

Add more crushed ice and stir again until thick.

Pour into a metal highball.

Add roughly broken ice for visual effect and garnish with the tip of a sprig of fresh mint leaves and a pipette of Cherry Heering, the best cherry liqueur. This will enable you to adapt the fruity and sweet aspect of the cocktail to your own taste. If you don't have a pipette, pour in the desired quantity of liqueur.

Very thirst quenching and slightly spicy, this cocktail brings out the aromatic flavours of the gin and is great served at any time of the day or night.

CACOGNAC

MAKES 1 GLASS

INGREDIENTS

15 ml (3 tsp) vermouth
15 ml (3 tsp) maple syrup
30 ml (1¼ oz) cognac
1 egg
spritz of cold brewed coffee
(or ½ tsp of filter coffee)
crushed ice

YOU WILL NEED
a shaker

Pour all the ingredients (except the ice) and crack the egg into the shaker.

Do a dry shake; in other words shake vigorously without ice to turn the mixture into an emulsion, then shake a second time after filling with ice.

Shake for a long time to cool the cocktail thoroughly, then filter into a large chilled coffee cup.

Spray the coffee on to the surface. To make the coffee extract, set 100 g (3½ oz) ground coffee mixed with 100 g (3½ oz) water to infuse for 24 hours in the fridge. Filter. If you don't have a spray, you can make the coffee into ice cubes and use them for the cocktail.

This creamy sweet cocktail can be served with a dessert or as a dessert in itself.

Pondicherry MULE

MAKES 1 GLASS

INGREDIENTS

50 ml (2 oz) vodka infused with cardamom seeds (put the seeds in the bottle and leave to infuse; the longer it is left to infuse the stronger the flavour)
20 ml (1 oz) lime juice
15 ml (3 tsp) sugar syrup
5 ml (1 tsp) ginger syrup
2 dashes of Angostura bitters
Fever Tree ginger beer
1 star anise
ice cubes

YOU WILL NEED
a shaker

Pour the ingredients, except for the ginger beer and star anise, into the shaker and shake vigorously until frost appears on the tumbler. Filter into a large highball type glass filled with ice cubes and top up with the ginger beer.

Decorate with the star anise and serve.

This fresh and slightly spicy cocktail is a thirst quencher at aperitif time and at any time in the evening.

EXPERIENCE
#3

MAKES 1 GLASS

INGREDIENTS

1 lemongrass stick
3 basil leaves
20 ml (1 oz) lemon juice
20 ml (1 oz) elderflower syrup
50 ml (2 oz) Pisco Waqar
crushed ice

YOU WILL NEED
a shaker

Cut a piece of the lemongrass stick, twist it to extract as much juice as possible, and put it in the shaker.

Add 2 basil leaves and pour in all the ingredients, then shake vigorously until frost appears.

Filter into a chilled cocktail glass and decorate with a basil leaf.

This fresh and slightly acidic cocktail brings out the floral flavour of the Pisco, and the sweetness of the elderflower will go down well at any time of the evening.

APPENDICES

Sauces
& BASIC RECIPES

PARSLEY BUTTER

- 200 g (7 oz) soft butter
- 2 bunches of parsley
- 4 garlic cloves

Peel the garlic, take the parsley leaves off the stalks. Blend the butter with the garlic and parsley until the butter is nice and green. You will only use part of this, and can freeze the rest; just form it into a roll and wrap in cling film (plastic wrap).

HAMBURGER SAUCE

- 50 g (2 oz) ketchup
- 1 tablespoon Dijon mustard
- 1 tablespoon HP sauce
- 1 tablespoon red wine vinegar
- 2 tablespoons peated whisky (such as Little Frog)

Thoroughly mix all the sauce ingredients.

BÉCHAMEL

- 60 g (2 oz) butter
- 60 g (2 oz) plain (all-purpose) flour
- 1 litre (34 fl oz) full-fat milk (whole)
- salt, pepper
- Espelette pepper nutmeg

Melt the butter then incorporate the flour with a whisk. When the roux (as this butter-flour mix is known) begins to change colour, remove from the heat. Bring the milk to the boil and pour onto the roux whilst whisking. Put it back on the heat and bring gently to the boil, stirring continuously until it has the consistency of a fairly thick sauce. Season with salt and pepper, the Espelette pepper and nutmeg.

SMOKY SAUCE

- 1 onion
- 1 tablespoon grapeseed oil
- 5 cm (2 in) fresh ginger
- 1 tablespoon honey
- 1 teaspoon Espelette pepper
- 200 ml (7 fl oz) water
- 3 tablespoons ketchup
- 2 teaspoons soy sauce
- 2 tablespoons liquid smoke (a liquid giving a smoky flavour, otherwise use barbecue sauce)

Peel the onion, cut into large slices, and chop the ginger. Gently fry the onion in the oil for about 10 minutes over a low heat to colour slightly, then add the ginger, stir, then add the honey. Allow to caramelize for 1 minute.

Add the Espelette pepper, the ketchup, the soy sauce, the water and the liquid smoke. Cook the mixture for 3–4 minutes until it is smooth and creamy.

COBB SALAD VINAIGRETTE

- 4 tablespoons olive oil
- 125 ml (4 fl oz) grapeseed oil
- 4 tablespoons red wine vinegar
- 2 tablespoons water
- ½ lemon
- ½ teaspoon of Worcestershire sauce
- 1 teaspoon Dijon mustard
- good pinch sugar
- good pinch salt
- good pinch white pepper
- 1 garlic clove, crushed
- ½ tablespoon maple syrup
- ½ tablespoon fish sauce (such as nam pla)

Whisk all the ingredients of the vinaigrette together (or put them into a jar with a tight lid and shake vigorously). You will have some vinaigrette left over for another recipe.

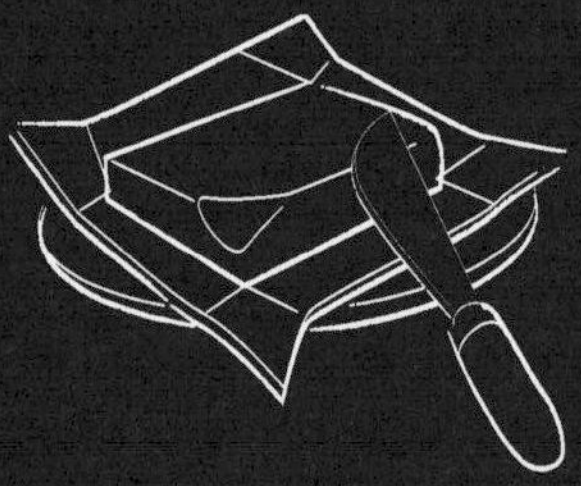

LEMON VINAIGRETTE

- *1 tablespoon wholegrain mustard*
- *1 tablespoon lemon juice*
- *1 tablespoon white balsamic vinegar*
- *1 tablespoon grapeseed oil*
- *1 teaspoon salt and pepper*
- *2 tablespoons walnut oil*

Whisk all the ingredients of the vinaigrette together (or put them in an air-tight jar and shake well).

GRAPE VINAIGRETTE

- *2 tablespoons balsamic vinegar*
- *3 tablespoons grapeseed oil*
- *3 tablespoons olive oil*
- *2 tablespoons grape must and walnut mustard (or a traditional wholegrain mustard)*
- *1 teaspoon salt*

Mix all the ingredients of the vinaigrette together.

TOMATO SAUCE

- *4 large very ripe tomatoes*
- *1 sweet onion*
- *2 sprigs of thyme*
- *2 bay leaves*
- *1 tablespoon tomato purée (paste)*
- *100 ml (3½ fl oz) olive oil*
- *salt, pepper*

Remove the stalks from the tomatoes and chop them with the skin on. Sweat the onion gently in the olive oil until transparent with the thyme, bay leaves and tomato purée. Brown then add the chopped tomatoes. Continue to cook for about 10 minutes. Do not cook for too long so that you keep the sauce as fresh as possible.

Add the olive oil and season.

SWEET CHILLI MAYONNAISE SAUCE

- *4 tablespoons mayonnaise*
- *½ bunch chives*
- *juice of 1 lemon*
- *1 teaspoon sweet chilli sauce (or replace with a smaller amount of ordinary chilli sauce, plus a large pinch of sugar)*

Prepare the sauce by mixing together the mayonnaise, the chopped chives, a dash of lemon juice and the chilli sauce. Adjust the seasoning to taste.

SPICY MAYONNAISE SAUCE

- *2 tablespoons mayonnaise*
- *a pinch of cumin*
- *1 tablespoon ketchup*
- *5 drops of Tabasco*
- *1 teaspoon soy sauce*
- *1 teaspoon fish sauce (such as nuoc mâm)*

Prepare the spicy mayonnaise sauce by mixing all the ingredients together.

MAYONNAISE SAUCE WITH OLIVES

- *100 g (3½ oz) mayonnaise*
- *juice of 1 lemon*
- *50 g (2 oz) pitted Kalamata olives*

Blend the mayonnaise with the olives, pass through a sieve to achieve a nice smooth consistency. Add a dash of lemon juice, adjust the seasoning to taste.

Sauces & BASIC RECIPES

HORSERADISH SAUCE

- *2 tablespoons prepared horseradish*
- *1 egg yolk*
- *120 ml (4 fl oz) sunflower oil*
- *½ tablespoon strong mustard*
- *salt, pepper*

Put the egg yolk, mustard and a little salt in a bowl. Whisk, adding the oil drop by drop, incorporating well as you go, then continue to pour in a thin stream, still whisking vigorously to create an emulsion. At the end, add the horseradish and pepper.

HOLLANDAISE SAUCE

- *4 egg yolks*
- *450 g (1 lb) butter*
- *salt*
- *4 teaspoons water*
- *the juice of ½ lemon*
- *Espelette pepper*

Clarify the butter by melting it gently; when it boils skim off the surface foam. Put the egg yolks, water and a pinch of salt in a saucepan. Put over a very low heat, whisking gently; when the mixture begins to smoke, whisk hard and scrape the bottom of the saucepan. Continue to cook, whisking the mixture well, until it increases in size, is smooth and even, with no lumps. It is ready when you begin to be able to see the bottom of the saucepan as you whisk. You may also find it safer to prepare this mixture in a bainmarie. Then gradually add the clarified butter away from the heat, whisking all the time. Add the lemon juice, a little salt if necessary and the Espelette pepper.

LENTIL SALAD

THE LENTILS
- *100 g (3½ oz) black beluga lentils*
- *4 gherkins*
- *1 tablespoon capers*
- *2 spring onions (scallions)*
- *½ bunch chives*
- *½ bunch parsley*
- *½ bunch chervil*

THE VINAIGRETTE
- *3 tablespoons sherry vinegar*
- *3 tablespoons walnut oil*
- *3 tablespoons grapeseed oil*

Cook the lentils in a large volume of water (starting with the water cold) for about 20 minutes; add salt midway through the cooking. They must be tender but still slightly firm. Drain them then add the onions, gherkins and sliced capers. Chop the herbs finely and add them to the lentils, along with the oil and vinegar.

FOCACCIA

- *250 g (9 oz) Manitoba pizza flour (or ordinary strong white bread flour)*
- *1 teaspoon dried yeast*
- *1 teaspoon salt*
- *1 teaspoon sugar*
- *180 ml (6 ½ fl oz) lukewarm water*
- *25 ml (1 fl oz), plus*
- *1 tablespoon olive oil*
- *1 tablespoon marjoram*
- *1 tablespoon rosemary*
- *1 tablespoon oregano*
- *a little plain (all-purpose) flour*

Mix all the dry ingredients in a large bowl. Add the oil and water and stir again. Knead the dough for about 15 minutes (or 10 minutes in a food mixer) until supple and elastic. Put the dough in a clean oiled bowl, cover with a tea towel or cling film (plastic wrap) and leave to rise for 2 hours; it should double in size. Knock down the dough and roll out into a rectangle on a floured worktop. Place on an oiled baking tray and leave for a further 20 minutes covered with cling film or a tea towel. Preheat the oven to 200°C (400°F/Gas 6). Brush the dough with a tablespoon of olive oil and bake for 15 minutes.

REMOULADE

- ¼ celeriac
- 1 head celery with the leaves
- 100 g (3½ oz) crab meat
- few drops Tabasco®
- 1 teaspoon white balsamic vinegar (or traditional balsamic vinegar but well sweetened)
- good pinch of sweet paprika
- 1–2 tablespoons of mayonnaise
- salt, pepper

Chop the celery into very small dice (brunoise) and snip the leaves. Mix together the crab, mayonnaise, vinegar, Tabasco and paprika, then season well.

BUNS

These measures make 10 buns; you can freeze any you don't use.

- 500 g (1 lb 2 oz) soft wheat white pastry flour, plus a little more for the worktop
- 2 teaspoons salt
- 30 g (1 oz) sugar
- 1 sachet of dried yeast
- 100 g (3½ oz) butter, at room-temperature
- 300 g (10 ½ oz lukewarm milk
- 2 eggs
- 2 tablespoons sesame seeds

Put the flour, sugar, salt and yeast in a large bowl or the bowl of a food mixer. Mix, add a beaten egg and the lukewarm milk. Knead by hand or with the food mixer at a slow speed for 10 minutes. Add the butter in cubes, knead again by hand or with the food mixer this time at a medium speed, for a further 10 minutes, until the dough comes away from the sides of the bowl. Cover and leave to rise at room temperature for 1 hour to 1 hour 30 minutes; the dough should double in volume. Place the dough on a floured work surface, divide into 10 pieces and roll them into balls as smooth as possible. Place the balls on a baking tray lined with greaseproof paper. Brush each bun with the second egg, whole and beaten, and sprinkle with sesame seeds. Leave to rise for 1 more hour. Preheat the oven to 200°C (400°F/Gas 6). Bake for about 20 minutes.

DRIED TOMATOES

- 4 medium-sized tomatoes, nice and ripe
- 2 garlic cloves
- 1–2 sprigs of thyme
- 1 teaspoon sugar
- 2 tablespoons olive oil

Put the tomatoes in a large bowl, pour on boiling water, wait for about a minute, then peel them. Cut into quarters and deseed. Preheat the oven to 65°C (150°F/Gas 1). Spread out the tomatoes on an oiled baking tray. Sprinkle with thyme and sugar, add the garlic cloves peeled, crushed and cut in half, sprinkle with olive oil and dry in the oven for 3 to 4 hours. You can also do this in a larger quantity and it will keep in the fridge for several weeks in a jar and covered with olive oil.

CARAMEL SAUCE

- 40 g (1½ oz) sugar
- pinch of salt
- 200 g (7 oz) full-fat single (half-and-half) cream

Put the sugar in a small saucepan, in a more or less even layer. Heat without stirring (shake the saucepan gently if necessary to spread the sugar out). When the sugar has melted and is beginning to turn golden, away from the heat add the cream and salt and whisk well to obtain a smooth sauce.

CHANTILLY CREAM

- 500 ml (17 fl oz) full-fat single (half-and-half) cream
- 40 g (1½) icing (confectioners') sugar

Mix the cream and icing sugar, pour into the siphon. Put in a cartridge and shake. If you don't have a siphon, whisk the cream until firm, add the sugar and whisk just enough to incorporate it.

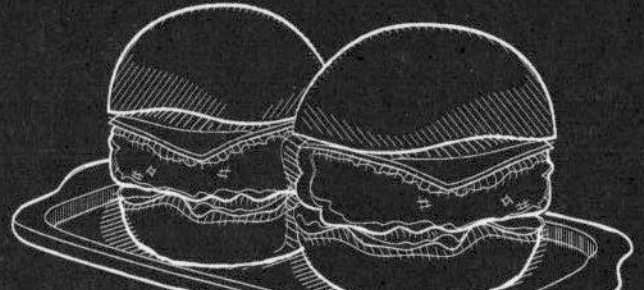

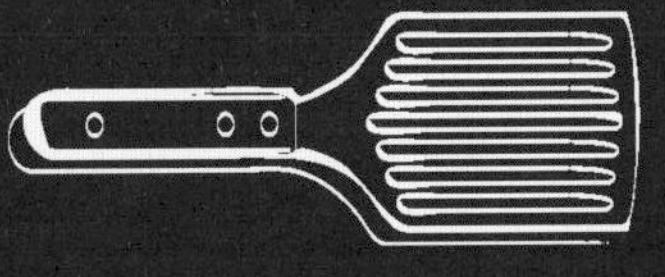

Index
TO RECIPES

BARBECUE

STARTERS

MAIN DISHES

SIDE DISHES

BRUNCHES

DESSERTS

COCKTAILS

SAUCES AND BASIC RECIPES

ACKNOWLEDGEMENTS

Creators of The Beef Club Olivier Bon, Romée de Goriainoff, Pierre-Charles Cros, Nicolas Chevalier, Jean Moueix.

Dorothée Meilichzon: designer and graphic designer.

Stephane Cunin: chef at The Beef Club, for the cooking and recipes.

Yves-Marie Le Bourdonnec: butcher.

Tim Wilson: cattle breeder.

Inko Garat and Charlie Brock: bartenders, cocktail masters.

the BEEF CLUB

58, rue Jean-Jacques Rousseau 75001 Paris
www.eccbeefclub.com

SHOPPING

Thank you to Brooklyn Tins and Piet Hein Eek
111, bd Beaumarchais 75003 Paris
www.merci-merci.com

Alcohol: please drink responsibly! As you know, drinking too much alcohol is dangerous to your health, so consume with moderation. We advise you to check official information sites, especially those related to alcohol consumption. You will find information on the law and on useful practices.

The Beef Club by Olivier Bon, Romée de Goriainoff, Pierre-Charles Cros, Nicolas Chevalier, Jean Mouei

Published in 2014 by Hardie Grant Books

First published in 2013 by Hachette (Marabout)

Hardie Grant Books (UK)
5th & 6th Floor
52–53 Southwark Street
London SE1 1RU
www.hardiegrant.co.uk

Hardie Grant Books (Australia)
Ground Floor, Building 1
658 Church Street
Melbourne, VIC 3121
www.hardiegrant.com.au

British Library Cataloguing-in-Publication Data. A catalogue record for this book is available from the British Library. British Library Cataloguing-in-Publication Data. A catalogue record for this book is available from the British Library.

ISBN: 9781742708034

Shopping: Sabrina Fauda-Rôle

Graphic design: Dorothée Meilichzon

Proofreaders: Jean-François Joubert and Pierre Jaskarzec

Copy Editor: Keda Black

Find this book on Cooked.

Cooked.com.au

Cooked.co.uk

Printed and bound in China by 1010

10 9 8 7 6 5 4 3 2 1